YOUR **HEART** WITH ALL DILIGENCE; FOR OUT OF IT FLOW THE ISSUES OF LIFE. WATCH OVER YOUR **HEART** WITH ALL DILIGENCE. KEEP THY **HEART**, FC

THE DI♥INE MATCHMAKER

LIFE. KEEP VIGILANT WATCH OVER YOUR **HEART** THAT'S WHERE LIFE STARTS. GUARD YOUR **HEART**, FOR IT AFFECTS EVERYTHING YOU DO. ABOVE A

JOEL & CASEY JOHNSON

Foreword by
Ron and Katie Luce

The Divine Matchmaker
— *God's a Matchmaker*

Published by Courtright
10716 Astor Drive
Keller TX 76244

ISBN: 978-0-9824967-9-4

Printed in the United States of America
with The Publishing Hub

RELIGION / CHRISTIAN LIFE / RELATIONSHIPS / LOVE & MARRIAGE

Contact the authors:

Joel & Casey Johnson
www.thedivinematchmaker.com

Acknowledgments

Thank you, Ron and Katie! Your family and marriage have been an inspiration to us! This book would not have been possible without the wisdom, advice, and love you've given to us over the years. Thank you for sacrificing your lives for this generation. Through your ministry, our lives have been changed! We are truly blessed!

(Casey) Thank you, Mom, you have been there for me through thick and thin. Our lives have not been easy, but we have persevered, and we are better people and friends because of it. I love you more than words can describe. You will always hold a special place in my heart. Thank you also to my Mimi and Papa. You have been an anchor in my life. I am who I am today because of your prayers, encouragement, and unconditional love. Your words of wisdom have guided me and I know you are always there, cheering me on to be better today than I was yesterday. I love you with all of my heart.

(Joel) Thank you, Mom, for loving me unconditionally. Grandma and Grampa, thank you for being a living example of what a lifetime of falling in love looks like. Grandpa, thank you for showing me how a strong man tenderly loves a woman.

Finally, we would like to thank all of our pastors, mentors, and friends who have invested into our lives and our marriage. We are honored to have walked alongside of you throughout the years.

CONTENTS

FOREWORD

If we could choose any couple to be a role model for how a relationship should be built, it would be Joel and Casey Johnson. We've known them since they were teenagers and they have become like our own. We have watched them as they began their internship at the Honor Academy, and we've watched them both grow up as a young man and woman. We've seen their whole process of friendship, courtship, engagement, and marriage; and now, they have graduated to parenting!

We are so proud of the stellar example that they have set for this generation. Because they have lived with such honor, God has promoted them to be able to influence thousands.

Joel and Casey both grew up in broken homes, but they were determined to have God's best and build their lives on His principles, because, after all, He is the only One who knows how marriage and relationships can work ... He invented them!

The greatest aspect of this book is that the writers themselves are living, breathing examples of how wisdom really works in relationships. They have got the most romantic, solid, and loving marriage on the planet, and it's because *they listened to wisdom crying out in the streets*" (Proverbs 1:20), applied it to their relationship, and now they are reaping the benefits.

If you want an awesome, wholesome, over the edge, out of the box, better than you could ever imagine relationship and marriage, read this book and do what it says! If you do what the world does, you'll get what the world gets—heartbreak, disillusionment, and divorce. But if you do it God's way, you'll get God's results.

— Ron and Katie Luce

PRELUDE:

FINDING A MATCHMAKER

"Two souls with but a single thought, two hearts that beat as one."

— John Keats

F inding true love is priceless. Wouldn't it be great if we all had someone, versed in the ways of love, to help us find it? That's what hundreds of men and women do on the hit reality TV show *The Millionaire Matchmaker*. For tens of thousands of dollars, millionaire bachelors hire Patti Stanger, the Millionaire Matchmaker, to help them find the only thing they haven't acquired: their true love. Patti has a massive index of the most eligible men and women in Southern California and boasts of having a 98% match success rate. Watch out eHarmony!

If we all had a matchmaker this successful to help us find Mr. or Miss Right, while avoiding Mr. or Miss Wrong, it might make some of us feel a little better about our chances of finding true love.

Although Patti's operation is impressive, wouldn't it be great to have a matchmaker who had an even bigger Rolodex than her? Let's say someone who had access to the most eligible individuals across the country or, for you international types, across the world? In addition, let's say this matchmaker was a personal family friend, had watched you grow up, knew pretty much everything about you, and offered you matchmaking help whenever you needed it. Wouldn't you feel better about your chances of finding your soul mate? I think we all would!

I hope it won't come as a surprise when I tell you that I employed someone much like this to help me find Casey, the absolute love of my Life. Without hesitation, I can say that the time, training, and money I invested totally paid off. Like my matchmaker told me, you can't put a price tag on finding everlasting love.

If you are single, you might be thinking you would be interested in getting his business card. (Even if you're not "in the market" right now, it might be good to have his contact info for some other time.) I promise, if you've seen the film *Hitch*, my matchmaker is the real life Alex Hitchens, only better. He's incredibly smooth—a true Love Doctor. He has helped even the most romantically-challenged individuals find their way down love's occasionally bumpy path. His staff services a 24/7 help line. He has a global database and connections everywhere. He is the world's foremost expert on love and a divine matchmaker. I relied upon His advice every step of the way and now I am hopelessly in love with the woman of my dreams. He led me into a romance with the right person at the right time and for that I am forever appreciative. Surprisingly, most people have heard of my matchmaker, but have no idea that He is so proficient in the art. You may be asking who this love guru is? His name is God.

While many lovers often believe they are truly a match made in heaven, few would go as far as to say that God, Himself, was their matchmaker. I think this may be an expertise of His that many grossly underacknowledge today, but is clearly attributed to God throughout the Scripture.

Abraham was a believer in God's keen matchmaking ability. This is undeniable. Just look at the instruction he gives to his servant sent to pick up a wife for his son, Isaac. He said, "*God will send his angel ahead of you to get a wife for my son*" (Genesis 24:7). Now if you've heard this story before, you might gloss over this verse and continue with the story. But if you stop and really think about what Abraham is saying, it is a bit bizarre. I've never heard anyone talk like this. I've never heard a pastor preach on this. Actually, if anyone did say to me that God's angel was going to pick out my spouse, I would probably recommend an excellent twelve-step program to him!

For most of us, the idea of winged angelic beings making people fall in love isn't totally a foreign concept, but we just expect to find this type of thing on Valentine's cards or in Greek Mythology, not in the Bible. So either Abraham was in need of some serious rehabilitation or maybe the person whom God called His "*good friend*" (Isaiah 41:8) was on to something.

The servant who was sent to get Isaac's "unknown" bride also believed God was a matchmaker. Abraham had instructed him to get a wife from Abraham's hometown, Nahor. The servant came to a spring outside the city where all the young ladies came to get water. He prayed that God would reveal the young lady to him by a specific sign; he would know it was her if, when he asked for a drink of water, she would not only give him a drink but would also offer to water all ten of his camels (an act that would take hours of labor to accomplish). When this happened, he would take it as a sign that God was "*working graciously behind the scenes*" (Genesis 24:14).

The servant knew God was at work—the Matchmaker was on the move—but he asked for God's help to uncover just who that person was.

As soon as the servant finished his prayer, he saw God begin to work. A *"stunningly beautiful"* girl came with her jug to draw water from the spring (Genesis 24:16). Her name was Rebekah. The servant asked her for a drink and she obliged him and then proceeded for the next few hours to water all of his camels until they had *"drunk their fill"* (Genesis 14:19). The servant silently watched her wondering to himself, "Was this God's answer? Had God made his trip a success or not?"

After she was done, the servant gave her five very expensive pieces of jewelry. Can you imagine Rebekah's delight? Her dinnertime spent serving at the well was rewarded with breakfast at Tiffany's! The Bible says she ran home to tell her parents (and if her neighborhood was anything like mine growing up, I would have ran too if I had been carrying that much bling).

The servant followed Rebekah to her house and discovered she was from the exact family from which Abraham desired his son to marry. He told them about the sign he had asked God for, how Rebekah fulfilled it by watering his ten camels, how he had prayed, *"Let [that] woman be the wife God has picked out for my master's son,"* and how God had worked behind the scenes to help him find the perfect match for Isaac. The family agreed and replied, *"This is totally from God. We have no say in the matter, either yes or no"* (Genesis 24:50). The next morning, the family asked the servant to let Rebekah stay a little while longer, but the servant said, *"Oh, don't make me wait! God has worked out everything so well—send me off to my master"* (Genesis 24:56, emphasis added). Rebekah's family asked her, *"Do you want to go with this man?"* (Genesis 24:56), and Rebekah replied, *"I'm ready to go"* (Genesis 24:58).

When Isaac met her, he fell completely in love. Rebekah had a ravishingly beautiful exterior, but her interior must have been just as captivating to Isaac because he let her wholly into his heart. Though there is not a lot of description of their early years together, we do know that after she came into his life something shifted in his soul. His heart became healthier. His life became richer. We know that at least one of the deepest wounds in Isaac's heart was healed through their union. Through Rebekah, Isaac's heart finally found *"comfort after his mother's death"* (Genesis 24:67). They were truly a match made in heaven.

If God is a matchmaker and knows everything about you, and everything about everyone, wouldn't He know who your perfect match is? If He's truly working behind the scenes trying to match you up with the right person, wouldn't it make sense to ask God for help uncovering who that person is? It worked out well for Abraham's servant and, ultimately, for Isaac and Rebekah. It might just work out well for you, too.

God's divine handiwork has united many hearts with their true love. This can be observed all throughout Scripture and attested to by many who have followed His matchmaking advice today. I followed His guidance and it worked out wonderfully for me. He brought me to my true love, Casey, and I can never adequately express my gratitude to Him for this.

In the pages ahead, we'll look at a few Biblical examples of the Divine Matchmaker at work, but mostly Casey and I will share our experience working with Him as He divinely orchestrated our love story. We'll definitely share some of His time-tested tips, secrets, and wisdom—so if you decide to use His services, you'll know how He works and be a little ahead of the curve. We really hope you'll use Him. There's no one who's been at it longer or is better at it than He. However, if you do choose to go with Him, you must remember that though His principles on love are timeless, He never brings two hearts together in the same way.

Here's to your match made in heaven! We hope you'll send us a wedding invitation.

— Joel and Casey

CHAPTER ONE

THE PROPOSAL

"You'll be the prince and I'll be the princess.
It's a love story, baby, just say, 'Yes.'"
— Taylor Swift, "Love Story"

"So, no matter what I say, what I believe, and what I do, I'm bankrupt without love."
— I Corinthians 13:3

"When somebody loves you,
It's no good unless he loves you — all the way."
— Frank Sinatra, "All the Way"

I don't know about you, but I am a real sucker for love stories. I enjoy snuggling up on the couch with a hot cup of tea and watching a romance movie that's a complete tear-jerker, and it's even better with a group of girlfriends. Just imagine it, girls all snuggled up together crying, Kleenex flying, and of course, bars of chocolate being eaten as if they had never been tasted before!

There is something about romance that takes my breath away—a man fighting for a woman's heart, and a woman fighting not to give it away too easily.

What is it about love stories that just gets us ladies all worked up? I think it's because we all hope for true romance. I think we put ourselves in the would-be lover's shoes, wondering how we would respond if we were in that situation. We each end up contemplating: "How would I respond if it were me ... if it were my heart being fought for ... oh, if I were the one being swept off my feet or rescued?" I have never met a woman who doesn't dream of that day, the day she meets Prince Charming, falls deeply—no, *madly*—in love, and lives happily ever after.

Every time I watch or read a love story, I cannot help but think back to my own love story. When I met my real life Prince Charming and fell deeply, madly, head-over-heals in love, I got the love story I had always wanted. So, snuggle up and grab a box of Kleenex as I tell you all about my love story ... and don't forget the chocolate.

Now, fellas (it's Joel here), this is no time to check out! As we share this story, you will find some indispensable gear you'll need, if you plan to successfully win the woman-of-your-dreams! So, lean forward, grab a Slim Jim and down a caffeinated beverage (or two), because you'll need every ounce of mental muscle to grasp how to capture and keep your dream girl's heart.

Several years ago, I was in California on Christmas vacation meeting Joel's family for the very first time. It had been a long two weeks and I was ready for a little time away. Joel's friends and family were amazing, but you have to understand, I was Joel's very first girlfriend, so you can imagine how nerve-wracking it was to meet his family that first time.

Believe me when I tell you, I felt like all eyes were on me. Joel was a 26-year-old, extremely handsome, very available (until I came along, of course) man of God, so there were many people who could not wait to meet the girl who had, finally, captured his heart. Wow … I felt there was so much to live up to! It was exciting, yet exhausting.

So, after nearly two weeks of meeting every one of Joel's family members and friends, I was in need of a break. Joel had thought of this, too. He had planned a little road trip with a group of friends, so we loaded up the car and headed to the beautiful beaches of Santa Barbara. Now, if you have never been to Santa Barbara, it is one of the most gorgeous places in California—perfect weather, perfect beaches, and perfect outdoor malls! We spent the first day shopping, shopping, and yes, more shopping (you've got to love those after-Christmas sales). I think I wore Joel out, so we took a little movie break and ended a perfect day in a cozy little coffee shop snuggled up by a fire.

(Joel, here again.) Yes, shopping had left me slightly fatigued, gentlemen. Navigating through hundreds of very determined women trying to get the last designer blouse or skirt, 50% off regular retail price (welcome to Southern California!) was enough to weary even the most robust of male mall shoppers. I was able to fight off the kryptonite effects of "bargain hunting" on this occasion for two paramount reasons. One, it was quite enjoyable watching Casey having so much fun and, two, I was madly in love with her and would have subjected myself to almost anything, even this shopping war zone, so that I could spend time with her. At that mall, in a very small way, I realized the precision of Pat Benatar's words, "Love is a battlefield!"

Joel had planned a nice little breakfast for me in Santa Barbara before we headed back to Sacramento. So, I got up early the next day, got dressed up, and we headed out for a little alone time. Now, Joel told me before we left for California to bring a nice dress because he wanted to take me out at some point during our trip. Believe me, I was looking forward to that all week long.

Our friends dropped us off at this remarkable five-star restaurant located on the beach. Joel, being the romantic guy that he is, pulled the table in front of a large window so we could enjoy the breathtaking view. After breakfast, Joel handed me a card.

Now, Joel had given me many cards throughout our relationship, so I thought nothing of it until I opened it. The card was a Jack Vetriano print, called *The Missing Man*. The card depicts a story you cannot help but get lost in: a woman in a white gown standing beside a woman in an elegant red dress, and behind the woman in red is a man with his arm draped securely around hers. The woman in white gazes into the distance for someone the artist leaves unknown to the viewer. I was immediately captured by the mystery the story told in this painting. Jack Vetriano is one of my favorite artists, so this card struck a heartstring. I could not wait to read what Joel had written inside:

> *Casey, you are truer than the North Star. You are the Rosetta stone ... decrypting the words of my heart, making sense of the impossible. Your heart is a bonfire; I am a man in the cold. I am so thankful I waded through four months of emotion to make sure I could hear the voice of God before I began pursuing you. I will always follow with a brave heart as the Lord leads and never take a step without Him. I thought I was going to die as I dove deeper and deeper down through my fickle feelings, but I am so glad I did not stop descending, because it was there, in the deep, where I found YOU—The Pearl of Great Price. Casey you are the highest price to be aspired, by men who are reborn. And here you are ... with me ... in my arms. Casey, I care for you with my whole heart. Thank you ... thank you so much for sharing your life with me right now.*
> *With my whole heart,*
> *Joel*

Wow ... where do I sign up? I'm sold! This man is amazing! Someone pinch me, I must be dreaming! After catching my breath, I tried to say something elegant and romantic in response, but let's face it ... I was pretty much speechless. What girl wouldn't be!? I attempted to describe how much the card meant to me, but failed to adequately communicate how dear the card truly was.

When I saw who the artist was, I started talking about another painting by him. You see, there is another Jack Vetriano painting, my favorite painting, *Dance Me to the End of Love*, it's called, which depicts a man in a tuxedo dancing with a woman in a white gown. The man's back is facing the viewer and only a partial silhouette of the woman's face is seen over his shoulder, leaving you to wonder what their relationship might be like. In the background, other couples (men in tuxedos, women in beautiful dresses) are also dancing, but the woman in the white dress is center-stage and is the focus of the painting. The painting gives you the feeling that this couple is all that really matters. You see their reflection in the wet sand they are dancing upon and it just captures you. I think one of the reasons I loved this painting so much, was that it compelled my own heart to contemplate what my special day and romance would be like. As I told you, I am a sucker for love stories!

After my less-than-direct response, Joel mentioned that he had a few last Christmas gifts for me. He gently pulled out a large gift carefully wrapped in silver paper. Now, throughout our courtship Joel would always give me sweet little gifts, most of which were picture frames of me and him, capturing special moments or places we had been. I did not mind the massive amount of pictures of us covering my room, but my roommate was less than amused. I could tell the gift was some kind of picture, and my mind automatically thought it was a giant size picture of me and him. While I was thrilled to receive a life-size portrait of me with the man I was madly in love with, all I could think was that my roommate was going to kill me!

I was as eager as a kid on Christmas morning and wanted to tear into the gift … but I refrained and opened the gift in a much more lady-like fashion. To my disappointment, I opened it with the picture facing away from me. As I turned the black frame over, I discovered that inside was my favorite painting. Girls, it was THE painting! Can you believe it? It was *Dance Me to the End of Love* by Jack Vettriano. I almost fell off my chair in disbelief. "Is this man real?" I thought to myself. "Better yet … is this man really mine?"

After, once again, catching my breath, I asked Joel how he had known. He said when he first met me I had mentioned the painting and how much I loved it. Well, he took mental note of it. Guys, pay attention … girls love thoughtful details!

Yes, this is when I (Joel) decided to capitalize on the accumulation of my thoughtful details thus far and said, "Casey, you are that woman in the white dress. You are beautiful, lovely, and

17

pure." Casey smiled as I stared deeply into her big, earnest, brown eyes.

Just when I thought it couldn't get any better, Joel said he had another gift for me. I was thinking, "Man, this is my lucky day. I LOVE gifts!" The next gift was just as carefully wrapped in silver wrapping paper with delicate silver ribbon and perfectly placed hearts across the box. Once again, I refrained from passionately ripping the wrapping paper off—after all, we were in public—so I carefully opened the box to find a beautiful white dress. I pulled it out of the box thinking, "This is a very strange gift." But I could not help but admire the beauty and simplicity of the gown. I kindly replied that it was a beautiful dress, but I could not keep from thinking that it was sort of a curious Christmas gift. Joel only added to my puzzlement by saying, "I have another gift waiting for you at the back of the restaurant, and you will need to take the dress with you."

At this point, I had no clue what was going on, but I am a sucker for gifts and, thus, anxiously proceeded to the back of the restaurant without further question. Joel has always been an exceedingly romantic guy, and I just thought he was going above-and-beyond on this one.

As I walked to the back of the restaurant, I noticed one of our friends standing in the back, waiting for me. Now, I was extremely confused! Providing no explanation, she took me to the restroom and instructed me to change into the dress. After I put the dress on, she handed me yet another neatly-wrapped gift. I began to put two-and-two together when I opened the silver wrapping paper and found a pair of white flip-flops. I got it ... we are going for a walk on the beach! Oh, if I only knew what was really in store for me!

After freshening up, I musingly walked back through the restaurant toward our table. It was then that I noticed Joel. He was sitting with his back toward me, just like I had left him, only something was different about him.

Forgive me (this is Joel), I have to cut in here, briefly. While Casey was changing, another friend of ours brought out a tuxedo I had rented. I ran to the other restroom and changed. The guy, who was paid to put soap on your hands and give you a towel when you are done washing them (seriously guys!), was staring at me with puzzled eyes. I ignored his snooty looks and ran back out to the table, hoping Casey hadn't beaten me back there. The table was empty and Casey was nowhere to be seen. I sat down and attempted to catch my breath before her re-arrival.

Ladies, as I walked toward the table I was amazed to see Joel, no longer wearing his casual clothes, but now dressed in a black tuxedo. I placed my hands on his shoulders. He stood up and turned around toward me, He looked so handsome! In his hands was another flawlessly-wrapped silver box. Inside was a pair of long white gloves that matched the dress.

Then all the pieces came together. I thought, "Here I am in a white dress with long white gloves, he's in a tuxedo ... this is just like the painting. "Wow, he is really going above and beyond this time." After helping me put my gloves on, he asked me if I would like to take a walk on the beach, and of course I agreed. We walked out of the restaurant, across the street, and to a set of stairs leading to the beach. As we proceeded down the stone stairs, I noticed red rose pedals strewn down them. As I got to the end of the stairs, I noticed more rose pedals covering the sand. Joel led me around the stairs to a private, romantic cove area on the beach. My eyes were roaming like a kid in a candy store, amazed at everything I saw in that cove.

First, I noticed the red and white-checkered blanket stretched out over the sand. There were candles lit and rose petals covering the blanket. My eyes were still taking everything in when Joel asked me to close them. I did, but I just kept thinking, "Wait, I haven't seen everything yet!" I wanted to take in this beautiful site as much as possible, and then I heard it. Its soft tone, dawdling tempo, and yawning melody was unmistakable. It was Norah Jones's *The Long Day is Over*, my absolute favorite romantic song.

I opened my eyes as I felt Joel's hands gently grasp mine. He pulled me close, slowly slid one arm around my waist, and then pulled me closer once more. We began to dance. This was the first time Joel and I had ever danced together. I will always remember it. As we danced, I slipped off my sandals. I soaked in the moment, the sound of the ocean breaking on the beach, the warmth of the sun on my shoulders, and the softness of the sand yielding under my bare feet.

After we danced for some time, Joel mentioned that he had another gift he would like to give me. He led me over to a big silver box sitting near the edge of the blanket. We knelt down together next to the box. I opened the gift and inside was a black book. Embossed on the cover, in silver, were the words, *To the End of Love*. Joel opened the book and began to read:

It was incredibly warm that night in October when it all began. Upstairs in her apartment, Casey was sharing her favorite verse in Isaiah when Joel saw something he had not seen before. In her eyes, he observed two miniature flames, which appeared and vanished like the flash of a firefly's tail. Joel's heart skipped a beat, if not two. Though what he saw lasted only a moment, it was long enough. Yes, long enough to awaken inside of him hope of the deepest kind. This deep hope, innate in man, is the same hope Adam had before the creation of Eve—the great desire to find a soul like your own.

From this time forward, Joel found himself desperate to know the origin of those flames, to know if the fire he caught sight of in Casey's eyes would unveil a heart made of the same. What Joel saw on that October night set in motion what would soon be the greatest discovery of his life.

Chills ran up and down my arms as Joel smiled at me and turned the next page:

After this, Joel's heart longed to be closer to hers, more than it ever had before. But he knew that if he were going to discover what her heart was truly made of, he would have to take great precaution, for her heart's sake and for his. He determined that he would not trust the blind instruction of his own frail feelings or leave it in the hands of chance. He made a commitment to God: He pledged he would not take one step without God's direction and would follow Him with a brave heart, wherever He would lead him. Joel was right. After setting up a score of barbeques, prayer meetings, and various other "group-get-togethers," he discovered the brilliant flames found in her eyes sprang from a heart of pure fire. A heart set ablaze by deep passion for her Lover, the fiercest King of all. Upon this discovery, Joel's heart did "jumping-jacks."

A fierce battle began to rage in Joel's heart. He wanted to pursue Casey with all that was in him, but he promised he would not take a single step without God's direction, but his own will, desire, and emotions were making it nearly impossible to hear His voice. It took Joel months of prayer to wade through the ocean of intense feelings he had for Casey. But he did not falter in keeping his vow to God; he was resolute in his decision not to pursue Casey until God clearly guided him to do so.

After nearly four months of mitigating his heart's overwhelming sentiment toward her, Joel, with the grace of God, finally subdued his will. For the first time in months, Joel's will, concerning this subject, was deeply and truly ready to do whatever God wanted without waver. Two weeks later, in January, he heard God speak to him and the Holy Spirit guided him to pursue Casey. Joel eagerly responded by following God's leading with a brave heart!

A few weeks later in Houston, Joel asked Casey out to lunch. Casey accepted. Lunch lasted seven hours. Two days later, January 27th, after traversing through a whole day of prayer and a sleepless night, Joel invited Casey out to coffee at Barnes & Noble. They walked around the store pursuing various portrait and photography books, but most of the time they spent talking and, more than they ever had before, laughing. Joel invited Casey to sit. They sat on the floor side-by-side, leaning against a tall oak bookshelf. As Casey and Joel looked through one particular book, which was filled with various photographs of lions and their cubs, Joel, finally, built up enough courage to ask Casey the question that he knew would lead him to defining his feelings for her. And so he asked, "What do you think the process leading up to a wholesome and godly courtship looks like?"

She said, "Oh?" and then thought for a second or two. She then answered, "Well, it would have to be a friendship that was centered around God."

Joel agreed and then asked her if she would like to enter into that kind of friendship with him. He nervously waited for a reply. She said, "Yes." Joel spent the next two days in a state of chemical imbalance.

Joel and Casey's friendship grew. They became closer … and closer … until they became best friends. Joel's heart grew more and more fond of Casey. And who could blame him? He had discovered the most wonderful, beautiful, and enchanting woman in the entire world. Once again, Joel sought God for his direction and guidance concerning Casey's and his relationship. One day, as he was praying in a field, he asked the Holy Spirit, "Do you want me to court Casey?"

The Spirit replied, "What do you want?"

Joel was momentarily stunned by the Holy Spirit's lively retort, but Joel began to thoughtfully and earnestly search the depths of his heart. What he discovered in his exploration was that there was nothing in the world he desired to do more. He exclaimed, "Yes! Yes, I want to court her!" He felt a great peace run over his heart like a strong and steady stream. That very day, Joel planned where and how he was going to ask Casey to court him.

On the morning of May 17th, Joel surprised Casey by cooking breakfast at her apartment and then whisking her off to Dallas for the day. They walked and talked for hours through what seemed like endless gardens at the Dallas Arboretum. In the center of the estate, Joel spotted a very curious-looking tree. It had an unbelievably thick branch that jutted, nearly horizontal, out from its lower trunk. The branch was only about two feet from the ground and had two drooping bows in it. Joel thought it seemed a perfect place to sit. So, he asked Casey if she would like to join him. She did and they talked some more and laughed much, much more.

In the midst of their conversation, Joel asked Casey what she thought the definition of a courtship was. After some thinking, she defined it to be a relationship with the possibility of marriage. Joel agreed and then, trying not to show his over-enthusiasm, asked her if she would like to enter into a courtship with him. She said, "I would very much like that."

They embraced and then prayed, dedicating their courtship to God. Throughout the ensuing weeks and months, Joel and Casey grew incredibly close. They began to care for each other more and more and more and more ... until they fell deeply in love. One year and two months after Joel discovered the flames of a heart wholly devoted to Christ, flickering in Casey's eyes, he got down on one knee, and for the very first time he told Casey that he loved her. He then asked her to marry him. Casey replied ...

Joel had stopped reading. My eyes were filled with tears as he tenderly asked me to stand. Joel then got down on one knee and pulled a little black box from his back pocket. (This was the kind of black box that houses a very particular piece of jewelry, one that I had dreamt of receiving since I was a little girl!)

My mind could not help but wonder what the ring looked like. It is an astonishing feeling, the anticipation I felt in my heart, waiting for that little black box to open. The words I had longed to hear my entire life were now coming out of Joel's mouth, "Casey, will you marry me?"

I must have drifted into a different world because I just stood there lost in his deep blue eyes. I was soaking up the moment when I detected a hint of concern in his gaze. I then realized I had neglected to answer him! While I was engrossed in the moment, with my head in the clouds, I had just left him there on his knee in suspense as to what I would say … I think he got a little nervous!

After realizing this, I shouted, "YES … YES, YES, YES, I will marry you!"

He quickly jumped from his knee, whisked me up into his arms, and spun me around. We danced one last time on the beach as we told each other over and over again how much we loved each other. After all, it was our very first time saying it!

Sorry to cut into the romantic flow of the story ladies, but I (Joel) felt it necessary to interject a thought here. Some people are shocked to hear that the first time I ever told Casey I loved her was after I proposed to her. The reason I had never said it before was that I didn't want to say those words to any woman I was romantically interested in without a commitment attached to it. I had seen too many relationships move too fast and then end in heartbreak. I had also seen the words "I love you" used by people to manipulate another's feelings. Usually it's the girl who feels the man is making a commitment, but he is really only using the words to get what he wants from the relationship. When I said the words "I love you" I wanted them to have weight and to really mean something. I wanted them to be attached to the commitment that I would spend the rest of my life with the woman who heard me say them. I wouldn't, and couldn't, use those words unless I truly meant them.

(Back to the story!) I didn't want that moment to end, but Joel said that he still had another surprise waiting for me. So, we loaded back up in our friend's car and drove to the Santa Barbara airport. I thought to myself, "Can this day get any better!" We arrived at the airport with just enough time to catch a flight to San Francisco. I then realized I had, in the midst of the romantic festivities, left my purse at the restaurant with my driver's license in it! We ran inside the airport to see if we could remedy this situation. Since Joel was in a tuxedo and I was in a white dress, they thought it was our wedding day, had compassion on us, and let me on the plane! Can you believe it? It seemed God was not going to let anything get in the way of my special day!

At that time, I boarded the plane with no idea where it was taking me ... and honestly, I didn't care. I was with the man I loved and with whom I was going to spend the rest of my life! The plane touched down about an hour later in San Francisco. Now, being a Texas girl, I had never been to San Francisco before, but had always wanted to visit. Joel had arranged for a different set of friends to pick us up from the airport and drop us off at Pier 39, one of the most famous attractions in San Francisco. After looking around the pier, we traveled over to Ghirardelli Square to catch a cable car. Joel bought us an all-day pass and we road up and down the hilly streets of San Francisco.

We stopped at Union Square, where there are malls, stores, shopping, and milling people all around. We ventured throughout the various shops and stores, Joel in his tuxedo and me in my white dress and sandals. In the midst of the romantic rush, I barely noticed the bite of the December air nipping at my bare toes, but at the mall I thought I should get them bundled up. I really did not feel like trekking around the city in heals, so I decided to trade in my flip-flops for fluffy white slippers from Bath and Body Works; after all, this was San Francisco, where almost anything is acceptable!

After our trip on the cable cars, Joel said he had one more surprise for me. We were both starving, so we grabbed a cab and headed off for dinner. We arrived at another pier and I noticed a large boat tied up to the dock. Joel led me onto the boat and I soon realized it was a dinner cruise around the San Francisco Bay! The cruise took you under the Bay Bridge and the Golden Gate Bridge. We had an amazing dinner, dessert, and then danced the night away to a terrific live jazz band. When the cruise ended, one of Joel's closest friends was waiting to take us back home. We sat in the back seat making wedding plans for the next hour and a half until we arrived back in Sacramento. I stayed at a friend's house that night and could not wait to call everyone the next morning to share the news. But before I did, I found myself just sitting in total amazement of God, at what He had done, and the man He had brought into my life.

I flashed back to my senior year in high school when I had made a commitment on a mission trip that I would not date until I met a man I thought I could marry. It was the hardest year of my life and one of the hardest commitments I would make. I remembered lying in bed and crying myself to sleep while all my friends were at the school dances, proms, or on dates with their boyfriends. I had faith that the Lord had something better for me, and that something better had just asked me to spend forever with him!

Though I endured many trials and had to wait many years before he came along, I was now, more than ever, thankful I did not give in ... that I did not give in to the peer pressure, temptation, and loneliness that had so many times tried to convince me to settle for something less than God's perfect desire for me. I just took a moment and thanked my heavenly Daddy. I felt like He was so near in that moment. I felt an overwhelming sense that I was His delight and He was just as excited about this day as I was. I thanked Him for giving me Joel, for giving me the strength to withstand all the years of waiting, and for giving me my dream proposal. It was all I could have hoped for and more!

I then sensed an irresistible knowing, a swelling in my heart, as if my heavenly Father was allowing me to experience how proud He was of me. I'll never forget it. It made all of those difficult years of being single on Valentine's Day, Christmas, and New Year's worth it. The memories of those lonely years were now replaced by the realization that I would never have to spend a holiday alone again. I was so glad I trusted my heavenly Daddy to bring me the right one at the right time.

I awoke the next morning and quickly glanced at my left hand .... I wanted to make sure last night was not a dream. The engagement ring was still there, and it was stunning. I just sat for about five minutes and marveled at how amazing my finger looked with a diamond on it, better yet, Joel's diamond on it!

We flew back to Texas that day, and I could not wait to announce to the world that I was officially engaged! When we arrived back in Dallas, all of my closest girlfriends were at the airport waiting to congratulate me. Joel suggested we stop at a particular restaurant to eat. We parked and walked inside. It was then that I noticed all of my best friends were already sitting at a table. The girls squealed and the guys yelled, "Congratulations!" We laughed, ate lots of food, and celebrated as I recounted the details of Joel's proposal. It was such an amazing moment seeing all of my best friends gathered around, celebrating such a special moment.

We had about a two-hour drive home from the airport. I was exhausted, but Joel said we had one more stop to make. He pulled into Ron and Katie Luce's home for one last little celebration. Ron and Katie have been like a mom and dad to both Joel and me and had played a large role in our relationship. They were waiting there with sparkling cider and roses to congratulate us. It was the perfect end to a perfect proposal.

Those two days contain some of the best experiences and memories of my life. I will never, ever forget them. Those two days showed me just how much I was loved by those around me, but more than anything, they showed me how much I was loved by the man with whom I was going to spend the rest of my life. This was the day every little girl dreams of, and he made my day a dream come true.

CHAPTER TWO

A Divine Rescue: The Quest for Casey

"It's news I'm most proud to proclaim, this extraordinary Message of God's powerful plan to rescue everyone who trusts him."

— Romans 1:16

"I know what I'm doing. I have it all planned out— plans to take care of you, not abandon you, plans to give you the future you hope for."

— Jeremiah 29:11

"Where there is love, there is life."

— Gandhi

My parents did not take me to church growing up, so when I became a Christian, I didn't know church etiquette. I didn't understand Church politics, what different religions believed, all the funny Christian-ese words, most of the stories in the Bible, and I definitely didn't understand the concept of modesty. To say I was un-churched was an understatement. I was the new girl in the youth group and I definitely looked like it! I remember feeling as if all the parents of the guys in the youth group did not like me. They would prefer that their sons date the girls in the youth group who were raised in the church as opposed to me. I can honestly now say, as a parent myself, I don't blame them for being cautious of me.

But unbeknownst to those parents, they made me feel like a complete outcast—a Jezebel after their perfect sons. If they only knew what those "perfect" sons were doing on Friday night, they would have probably been a little slower to gossip about the speck in my eye. Their judgments cut me to the core. I thought I was undeserving of a good Christian guy. Because of my past mistakes and because I was not raised in a Christian home, I thought I was somehow disqualified from the man of my dreams. An amazing man of God was only deserving of an awesome woman of God, void of mistakes, and perfect. I was not her.

Years later, I began to fully understand how Christ viewed me. Though I was once stained as red as crimson, I was now washed white as snow, fully deserving the absolute best God had for me. Though I now understand that, I cannot help but think of the thousands of girls and guys who believe their past mistakes have disqualified them from God's best. That is not true!

Every little girl, and every grown woman for that matter, dreams of her Prince Charming. What will he be like? Will he be tall, dark, and handsome or blonde with blue eyes? We dream of that perfect day with our perfect man, yet somewhere along the way we trade our dream of Prince Charming in for a frog.

Now, many of us ladies have dated a few frogs along the way, settling for less than what we deserve (if you have not dated one of these amphibians, consider yourself blessed). Many of us girls have made mistakes along the way and our hearts have the scars to prove it. I have talked to numerous girls who feel they must settle for less because they have been less than perfect.

You might be saying, "But Casey, you don't know my past. You don't know the mistakes I have made, the pain I have been through." While I may not know your particular story, I know the goodness of a heavenly Father who picks us up, dusts us off, forgives us, heals our wounds, and gives us a fresh start. To fully understand where I am coming from, I guess you have to know my story.

My childhood was not perfect and like most kids I blamed myself for its imperfections. I didn't grow up knowing what it was like to have two parents in the home. Honestly, I didn't know what it was like to have two parents who got along! My mom and dad divorced when I was only a year old and ongoing fights between the two of them were all I ever knew. Custody battles and courtrooms were normal to me. I grew up understanding the meaning of child support, visitation rights, and the term "dead beat dad." I grew up thinking those things were normal. I remember courtrooms and my mom coaching me on what to say to the judge so she would get custody of my two older brothers and me. There is much of my childhood I don't remember, probably traumatic things that I have blocked out, but the things I do remember have left deep wounds in my life.

I must preface this by saying that I get along great with my mother now. She has made many mistakes in her life, like we all have, but we have moved on. She is a wonderful woman and mother and we have chosen to put the past behind us. I love my mom with all my heart and could not imagine my life without her, but to fully understand me, you must know a bit more about me.

When I was about 5 years old, my mom re-married. She was 29 with three kids, and her new husband, Brian, was only 18. As you could imagine, it was a less than an ideal situation. I don't remember much about Brian, except that he was verbally abusive to my brothers, probably because the stepdad role didn't come easy to an 18-year-old. Needless to say, that marriage didn't last long and there was another nasty divorce.

One of my most vivid memories of this divorce occurred when I was probably seven years old. Late one evening, Brian came over to the house to discuss the divorce with my mom. He walked through the front door and down the hall toward their bedroom. Me being a nosy 7-year-old, I crept down the hall to listen in on the conversation. As their discussion became more heated, I peered around the corner to catch a glimpse of what was going on. I saw Brian with a gun pressed against my mom's head, threatening to pull the trigger. I frantically rushed to our neighbor's house and pounded on the door until they answered.

With tears streaming down my face, I managed to mumble out the words, "He has a gun and is going to shoot my mom!" The neighbors immediately called 911 and within a few minutes the cops arrived. I stayed at the neighbor's house until I saw the police load my stepdad into the back of the cop car and haul him away.

Fortunately, my mom was OK, but that wasn't the last time we saw him. Obviously, he didn't have a change of heart in jail, because a few days later he was back! It was a school day. My mom was at work and she had allowed us to stay home to watch the house in case he returned. Since when does a kid turn down an opportunity to miss school? My brothers and I gladly accepted the challenge! After all, I was a 7-year-old force to be reckoned with. I may not have been able to fight him off, but my fingers sure could dial 911, and rather quickly, too. There is something about those three numbers that just peaks your curiosity at that age!

So, there we were, at home, rebels skipping school to play lookout for our psycho stepdad. I was in the kitchen when I heard a window break in the garage. I opened the door leading to the garage and peeked inside and saw Brian! He had smashed the small windows at the top of the garage door and was pulling the emergency string to open it! I ran into the living room to get my brothers and yes, finally had an opportunity to dial 911! I don't remember if the police got there in time. Brian didn't stay long after he realized my mom had changed the locks on the truck that was parked in our garage.

To this day, my mom still swears she married him because she needed a babysitter while she was at work! I would have preferred daycare. While my mom pretended she didn't care about him and that the divorce didn't hurt her, I knew it did.

One weekend, after my brothers and I spent time with our real (biological) dad, I remember seeing what looked like enormous cuts up my mom's arms. When I asked her what had happened, she said, "Brian did this to me." At the time I thought my stepdad had cut her arms, but I later realized my mom had tried to commit suicide. I remotely remember visiting my mom in the hospital. I didn't fully understand what kind of hospital it was, but I learned later that it was a mental institution.

After my mom's second divorce, things in the house changed dramatically. I knew my mom enjoyed the party scene before her second marriage, but I was too young to fully understand what was going on. However, this time around, I fully understood what was happening. My mom was hitting the clubs for what seemed like seven nights a week, and each night it seemed like she would bring a different guy home with her. I remember elaborate dresses, jewelry, shoes, make up, and I can't forget the friends she would bring along with her. Each night I would watch my mom get ready for the clubs and each morning wake up with a different guy in our house.

My mom would often be too tired to get me dressed, so my brothers and I would get ready by ourselves and walk to the bus stop. You could imagine what a 7-year-old girl looks like when she gets herself ready. I was a mess and still have the school pictures to prove it!

My mom had a few consistent guys in her life, but those relationships didn't last very long. I recall one guy my mom was especially hung up on. His name was Robert, and I remember really despising him and his little group of friends. It started out as a usual night of clubbing for my mom, Robert, and their friends, but this night ended rather abruptly. Typically, I was in bed asleep by the time my mom got home; but this night she came home unusually early and brought along this group of friends. My mom was crying uncontrollably and her friends were trying to calm her down. They eventually got her into bed, but she kept crying out, over and over again for her boyfriend Robert.

I had never seen my mom like that, and looking back I now realized my mom was extremely drunk. I was a complete momma's girl, so when I saw my mom like that, fear gripped my heart! I could not believe what I was seeing and had no idea why she was so upset. It seemed like a complete circus in our house and these friends were frantically looking for my mom's keys to hit the clubs again! As I lay in bed with my mom, trying to calm her, I remember her telling me not to give them the keys to her truck. I quickly took her keys and hid them in the tank portion of the toilet. (Having two brothers teaches you to hide things really well and it was especially handy in situations like these.)

My mom's friends never found the keys and finally had to call someone else to come and pick them up. As a child, seeing my mom in that state was forever burned in my mind.

My mom's habitual dating and club life continued until she met the man who would soon become her third husband, Adrian. He was a truck driver passing through and it seemed to be love at first sight. If I remember correctly, she had known him for a few days when she decided to spend a week with him on the road. She packed up and away she went, leaving her three kids home alone to fend for themselves. I was still around seven at the time, my brothers were a couple of years older, and while I didn't mind being left at home alone, I am pretty sure the law would have had something different to say about it had they known. After three consecutive days of missing classes, my grandma received a phone call from our school. She phoned the house and realized we were alone. I reassured her we were fine and requested that she bring us some of my favorite Braum's cookies. My grandma would check in on us on a consistent basis, but was terrified to take us for fear that my mom would call the police on her. She was trying to avoid us ending up in foster care.

Shortly after my mom returned, she packed up our entire house and moved us to Dallas to live with her new "Romeo." Soon after, they married and I had a new stepdad. Life was pretty smooth for awhile. They loved each other and my brothers and I were learning to adjust to a new life. After a few years of marriage, their love-at-first-sight faded. Adrian would be gone for weeks at a time, driving truck, and it was not long before my mom developed an interest for a man where she worked. Before I knew it, this new guy was coming over to the house and spending the night while my stepdad was away.

You have to understand, I was so young and my mom's lifestyle was all I knew, so I didn't understand the concept that people do not have relationships with other people while they are married. I didn't understand that what my mom was doing was wrong. All I knew was, "No matter what, do not tell Adrian!" After all, I liked the new boyfriend much better than my stepdad!

Things seemed to be going smoothly for my mom until one day the phone bill came in the mail. My mom realized there were several calls to an unknown number. I recall sitting on the couch watching my mom as she curiously phoned the number on the bill. She soon realized it was the number to my stepdad's girlfriend. Looks like my mom was not the only one with a drifting heart!

The truth was out, and my mom's heart was torn to pieces. My mom cried uncontrollably as she realized her third marriage was over. Instead of divorce, my mom and stepdad attempted to work things out, but they knew that would not be possible with him on the road and her at home. So, she decided to move her life into the back of an 18-wheeler, but there was just one problem—there wasn't room for the three of us kids! It seemed like my life was changing right before my eyes. The woman I admired, adored, and loved with all of my heart no longer had room for me in her life. Within days it was arranged that my brother and I would go to live with our real dad.

I loved my dad very much, but I had spent my entire life living with my mom. To say that I was terrified would be an understatement. I stood at the end of the circle drive, with tears streaming down my face, watching my mom drive away in that large 18-wheeler. I stood in the street until I could no longer see the truck in the distance. Later that night, I remember paging my mom. When she returned my phone call, I told her how I didn't want to live with my dad and begged her to come back and pick me up. The words she said back to me were like a dagger to my heart, "We are too far away to turn back now and get you." I was crushed. It felt as if my heart was broken into a million pieces.

A few days later, my dad pulled into the driveway to pick us up and a new chapter of my life began. I wish I could say it was a wonderful one, but unfortunately it was not. My brothers and I moved to Oklahoma to live with my dad. Life with my dad, stepmom, and half-sisters was completely different than what we were used to. My dad was extremely strict and tried to provide rules and structure to our broken lives, but the world we knew had been shattered. We felt like intruders into a somewhat perfect family.

It took some time to adjust to a new family, new school, and a whole new world, but I got along great with my stepmom and sisters, and I even started making good friends at school. I was trying to adjust the best I knew how, but my mom was having a difficult time allowing that. She didn't want us, but she didn't want us to be happy with our dad, either. Every time my mom would call, it seemed like my heart shattered all over again. The conversation would be filled with her empty promises and hatred toward my dad. After talking to my mom on the phone, it seemed like all the progress I had made was destroyed.

I recall one specific phone conversation I had with my mom. She had somehow found out that I had told my stepmom that I loved her. I remember my mom telling me that you could only love one mom, not two, and I needed to choose which mom I loved.

My 11-year-old mind was unable to comprehend the statement. I absolutely adored my mom, so needless to say, that was the last time I told my stepmom that I loved her. My dad noticed such a dramatic change in us after our talks with our mom that he felt he needed to know what he was dealing with. He became so concerned over what my mom was saying to us that he installed a phone recorder without our knowledge so he could hear our conversations. I had a lot of good memories during those days, but it seemed like every possible good memory was shattered by fights between my mom and dad. I felt like I was constantly being torn between the two of them. When I was with my dad, it was wrong to love my mom, and when I with my mom, it was wrong to love my dad.

When I was 14, my mom and Adrian moved to Oklahoma, where my brothers and I were living with my dad. I remember sitting at the kitchen table with my two brothers and my dad. With tears streaming down his face, he gave us the option of living with him or with my mom. After being away from our mom for nearly three years, we all chose to live with her.

I wasn't a little girl anymore; I was a teenager now, and soon began to realize that my mom wasn't as perfect as I had remembered her. I also saw how broken my life really was. My childhood had not been normal. I had been through so much in my 14 years of life and had found my own ways of dealing with everything. In my 8th grade year, I started hanging out with a bad crowd and experimenting with alcohol.

It was also during my 8th grade year that my mom's third marriage started to fall apart. I would walk to my mom's work after school and my stepdad would pick us up after her shift. One day he did not show up and when my mom called his work, she discovered he hadn't come in that day. My mom and I walked almost five miles home. When we arrived, he and all of his things were gone. Words cannot describe the emotional breakdown that ensued. I hated seeing my mom that way, her heart again shattered into a million pieces. She had given up so much, even her kids, to make that marriage work, and one day he was gone and the marriage was over.

But this was not my mom's first heartache, nor her first divorce, and with some time, her heart recovered. Before long she was out on the town looking for a new man to fill the empty void. It seemed like night after night she was at the clubs and a new flow of guys would be in and out of her life. Before long, she was in love again, but my stepdad, Adrian, though completely out of her heart, was not yet out of her life. He rolled back up to our house one day and explained to my mom that he had made a mistake, and boom, he was back in her life and our house.

There was only one problem: She was still dating this other guy. So, once again, the cycle repeated itself, as my married mom dated another man. It was not long before my stepdad found out, and this time the marriage was really over. That was the last time I saw Adrian, and in a short time, her new romance was in full swing. While sleazy does not quite describe how disgusting this guy was, my mom's excuse was that he was a good dancer and she loved him.

My freshman year provided even more opportunities to experiment, which is exactly what I did. High school was a whole new world that offered plenty of opportunities to forget about your home life. I got lost in the world of popularity, parties, drugs, and alcohol. I was a cheerleader and enjoyed playing sports, but football games and track meets where filled with bittersweet memories.

One of my fondest memories was at a cross country meet. I was living with my dad at the time, and he, my stepmom, and stepsister attended my first meet of the season. I remember running out of a wooded area of the trail, and as I rounded the corner, out of the crowd I saw my dad's face cheering me on. He ran with me the last half mile to the finish line and gave me a gigantic hug after I finished. Even though we had a great time that day and my dad's heart was full of pride, I could not help being sad that my mom was not a part. Oftentimes my dad would not attend my sporting events when my mom would be there because a fight between the two of them was almost inevitable. I felt that if I was showing affection to my dad and stepmom, I was alienating my mom, and vice versa. There was not a single event that I simply enjoyed because in the back of my mind, I always wished my dad was there to watch me succeed.

While my dad did not miss any of my stepsisters' softball games, he was not too fond of the fact that I was a cheerleader, so he never attended any of my events. He would go to the high school football games, but sit on the opposite side of the cheerleaders. My mom, on the other hand, was at every single pep-rally and would come to the first half of every football game. She would leave early with her boyfriend to hit the clubs, but no matter how late she stayed out the night before, she would never miss the track or cross country meet the next morning. I know my mom was not perfect, but that is one thing I always appreciated about her. She was always there to cheer me on. Some of my favorite memories were going out to eat after the meets and listening to music on our drive home.

I spent much of my high school life bouncing back and forth between my mom's house and my dad's house. While I loved my dad very much, I often felt as if I didn't quite fit into his family. Like I said, he was remarried with two daughters and I felt like I was just a nuisance from his previous marriage. The countless fights that transpired between my mom and dad over me and her endless threats on my stepmom's life eventually wore my dad thin. I felt that to fit in with my dad's new family, I had to hate my mom and alienate her from my life, which was impossible. Although I had a difficult time accepting my mom's lifestyle, she was still my mom and I loved her very, very much.

Often times, my stepsisters would get preferential treatment, which really made me feel like I was not a part of the family. Some of the most hurtful memories were times that my stepsisters would come home with hundreds of dollars worth of clothes, yet I would have to argue with my dad to just get a winter coat. Though I desperately needed braces as a teenager, I was never even taken to a dentist, yet my dad paid for my younger stepsister to get braces. If I wanted $20 to go to the movies, I had to spend the entire day cleaning my dad's shop, while my stepsister didn't even have to blink an eye to get whatever she wanted. My mom was struggling to make ends meet, yet she still managed to buy me school clothes and glasses. My dad was extremely hard on me and my brothers, and that only caused me to rebel.

However, looking back, I am so thankful for my dad's stringent rules and standards. I am who I am today because of them, but as a teenager I didn't understand them. My dad spent so much time at work and out of town that it left little room for a relationship with me. I have heard it said that rules without relationship produce rebellion, and that is exactly what happened. The harder my dad was on me, the more I rebelled.

I remember one night at my dad's house after he and my stepmom had been drinking. My bedroom was right off of the living room and it was late, but I overheard them talking. My stepmom was saying how she wished I were not a part of the family. She felt that every time I returned from my mom's house that I was acting just like my mom. She wished it was just her, my dad, and my two stepsisters. As I lay in bed that night, crying myself to sleep, I could not help but feel completely unwanted. The next day, I packed my things and moved in with my mom. Once again, I remember my dad sitting with tears in his eyes at the kitchen table, watching me walk out the door. I was angry and broken and this was just the beginning of my life spinning out of control.

There I was, back at my mom's house, and it was more broken than ever. My dad was the type of man who had no use for you if you were not doing what he thought you should be doing. Months and months would go by, and I wouldn't see my dad. I would try, in my own way, to reach out to him, but all I felt was rejection and disappointment from him. He would visit his friend who lived across the street from me and see me in the front yard, but not even a simple hello would emerge from his mouth. He treated me like an adult, but I was just a broken teenager trying to work out my own issues.

There was a new-found freedom in my mother's home. While my dad had a rule for everything, my mom had no rules, at all! My mom would spend the weekends at the clubs and I would spend the weekends with a house full of people, partying our lives away. My brokenness, insecurities, and unstable home life led me to search after any superficial thing I could find to fill the broken, empty space inside me. Parties, popularity, and boyfriends provided a temporary fix, but I knew something was missing. It seemed that the more I partied, the more guys I dated, the more popular I became, the more and more empty I felt on the inside.

It was my junior year of high school when I hit rock bottom. It was New Year's Eve and my friends and I began the night at my house. We were completely drunk when we headed out of town for the big party of the night. We arrived with our own share of liquor, but there was already plenty to go around at this party. This party was completely out of control. There were a lot of people I knew and many I didn't know. I remember getting so drunk and high that I spent half of the night hovered over the toilet. At one point, I remember feeling as if I was completely out of control. The reality of my decisions hit me hard when I realized anything could happen to me and I would have no way of stopping it.

I woke up the next morning with a sick feeling in my stomach. The reality of what could have happened to me hit me like a load of bricks. For starters, my friends and I were completely trashed when we drove to the party and when we drove home. We could have killed ourselves, or even worse, killed someone else. I had been to many parties in the past, but I had never been to a party like this, and I had never consumed that much alcohol! The realization that absolutely anything could have happened to me sent chills down my body.

I was contemplative as I realized how serious things had become. Was this really all there is to life? Was this really the best way to deal with my problems? No matter how popular I was, no matter how cute my boyfriend was, and no matter how drunk I was, the pain in my heart still remained. And so began my journey to find freedom! I didn't know what I needed, but I knew I needed something.

Around that same time, a friend of mine invited me to a youth event called Acquire the Fire. (This is where the story gets good!) I had never been to a Christian event before and was not raised in church, so this was a whole new experience for me. As I entered the smoke filled arena, my mouth dropped to the floor. This was not what I expected out of a Christian event. I was surrounded by breathtaking rays of lights, over-sized video screens, a colossal stage, and thousands of teenagers shouting FIVE, FOUR, THREE, TWO, ONE!

My heart leaped out of my chest as the boom of the pyrotechnics filled the arena and sprays of fireworks blinded my eyes. The music began and immediately my heart was captured. I watched as an arena full of my peers stood to their feet and eagerly joined in with the music. I noticed there was something different about the music and about these teenagers. My eyes were glued to the thousands of people, standing to their feet, with their eyes closed and hands raised as they sang passionately to their Creator. I had always believed in God, but did not know that this type of relationship with Him existed. Tears filled my eyes as I realized they had what I wanted and was searching for so desperately.

Though I didn't give my life to the Lord that weekend, a curiosity was sparked inside of me and a glimmer of hope began to grow in my heart. If what I saw and heard at that event was true, then I knew Jesus was exactly what I needed. I embarked on a journey to discover more about Christianity and this Jesus character. I began attending a local youth group and before I knew it, I felt right at home. I had heard about mission trips at Acquire the Fire and desperately wanted to go when an opportunity presented itself through my youth group. We would be taking a youth trip to Houston, Texas to work with an inner-city church, and I was the first to sign up!

The week was full of daily activities, outreaches to the homeless, playing with kids at a women's crisis center, painting houses in the inner city, and many other ways of serving the community. Our nights were full of worship sessions and various teachings from different pastors, but one night meeting in particular had a major impact on me. I don't remember what the message was about, but I felt a deep longing in my heart to respond. I had a moment with God that night that I will never forget. For the first time in my life, I felt like God saw right through me. He saw through the insecurities masked in partying and popularity. He saw through to the depth of my heart, the hurt and pain I had endured throughout the years—the years of longing for love and acceptance from my father, the years of wanting, just one time, for my mother to choose me over her boyfriend—a want that always left me disappointed. He saw all of the many mistakes I had made and regrets I carried, yet He loved me and accepted me for exactly who I was.

For the first time in my life, I didn't care what people thought. I wasn't worried about what my friends thought or what the youth group thought. I only cared what God thought of me. In that moment, surrounded and captured by God's love, I surrendered my entire life to Him. It seemed like I spent hours at the altar that night and when I got up from my knees, I was different. I was free. That was only the beginning of a pursuit of reckless abandon after God's heart. I was madly, deeply, head over heels in love with my Creator, and I would stop at nothing to get more of Him.

The next night, I felt God calling me to pull away and spend some time with Him. I found a quiet little place away from the youth group, got on my knees, and began to cry out to the Lord. I felt God speaking to me that for so many years the world had a hold on my life. I was a product of pop culture. I had spent years trying to be like the girls on the cover of magazines, in MTV videos, and in the latest hot TV series. I felt the Lord telling me that if I did not remove those things from my life, they would always have a hold over me, so I made a decision in that moment with God that I was really going to do this Christian-living thing. It was all or nothing. I committed to the Lord that for one year I was not going to watch TV or movies or listen to secular music, only Christian music, and I was not going to date until I met a guy worthy of my heart.

I know this sounds a bit radical, and it probably was, but I knew if I did not make a deep commitment to serve God with all of my heart that I would always be a lukewarm Christian.

I returned home from that mission trip a different girl. I took the television out of my room, threw away my movies, and burned all of my secular CDs. I broke up with my many boyfriends, and if guys called me, I would tell them they could hang out with me on Wednesday night at youth group!

I was entering into my senior year of high school. I was still a cheerleader and knew these commitments would not be easy, but I wanted God more than comfort. Cheerleaders were required to attend high school dances after the football games, so I met with the coach to be excused from all dances, but still came once the dances ended to clean up, which was also part of the cheerleaders' responsibilities. I did not attend my senior prom, which was hard, but I don't regret it. To be honest with you, my senior year was one of the hardest years of my life. There were many lonely nights when my friends were on dates, at dances, or yes, even the prom, while I was hanging out at home with my Bible, but I knew someday it would all pay off. Boy did it ever!

Shortly after I returned from my mission trip to Houston, I signed up to go on a trip with Teen Mania Ministries over Christmas break. I knew my life was going to change on the trip, but I never anticipated the magnitude to which it would. On December 26th, hundreds of teenagers, passionate about God and missions, met at the Dallas/Fort Worth airport for the beginning of our trip. After all of the teenagers arrived, we loaded onto large white school buses and headed to our final destination: New Orleans, LA.

After many hours in the buses, the once enthusiastic teenagers were now sleep deprived and cranky after being cramped in overloaded school buses that smelled like dirty feet and sweaty armpits. Yuck! Needless to say, we were all relieved when the buses finally pulled into the gas station and slowly came to a stop. We were hoping for a much needed bathroom break, but to our disappointment, we were told no one could get off the bus. Confusion and a little bit of frustration filled the overcrowded bus until our team leader stood up and asked if there was a Casey Wolston in the group.

"Wait a second," I thought, "that's me." I raised my hand and was then instructed to step off the bus and follow them. I was terrified! A million thoughts raced through my mind, "Did I break a rule? Was I in trouble?" I wanted to discover why I was being singled out among hundreds of teenagers and was partly relieved when I was told that I needed to make a phone call home. I stepped up to the pay phone and made the call that would forever change my life.

My mom answered with a quiver in her voice. I could tell right away something was wrong. She began to explain that her teacup poodle, Precious, had died and she had just finished burying her in the back yard. I unsympathetically replied, "You did not just pull me off of a bus in the middle of my trip to tell me that your dog died!" Unfortunately, that was not why I was pulled off the bus. My mom then explained that my dad had been in a motorcycle accident and I needed to come home. She said he was in the hospital, but thought it was best that I return early from my trip.

A million questions flooded my mind as I pressed my mom for answers. She just kept responding, "Casey, you need to come home." As I hung up the phone, I burst into tears. I was completely devastated. Not only was I worried about my dad, but I also did not want to leave my trip early. I had worked so hard for this trip, I had spent months fundraising and praying for the people of New Orleans, and just like that, it was over.

I sat in the front seat of the bus with my team leader, Heather, for the remainder of the drive to New Orleans. I don't think I could have survived that day without her. She didn't know anything about me, but she did know the situation that awaited me at home. She prayed and sang worship songs over me as I lay my head in her lap and cried the rest of the way. Deep down inside I thought my dad was going to be fine. I kept explaining to the team leaders and project directors that I served a big and mighty God and that He could heal my dad. My faith could have moved mountains that day.

When we arrived in New Orleans, my bags were loaded into a rental car, and I was driven to the airport. I was eager to see my dad and imagined we would go to the hospital as soon as I arrived home. My mom was there to greet me at the gate when I arrived in Oklahoma City. It seemed like a quick drive home and as we pulled into the driveway, I bolted out of the car and into the house. I could have never imagined the news awaiting me when I walked through the front door. My house was full of people, which wasn't unusual, and my oldest brother, Cory, was standing in the doorway. In the midst of a big hug, I asked him, "How's Dad?"

He said to me, "Casey, Dad's gone. He didn't make it." In that moment my whole world was shattered into a million pieces. I dropped to the floor in complete disbelief. Is this really happening to me? I felt as if I had been caught up in a tornado and was waiting for it to take me back to Kansas.

After my total emotional meltdown in front of the crowd of people at my house, my brother took me to my room and explained everything to me. I was extremely confused and had been told so many different stories. My brother began to explain that my dad had actually passed away at the scene of the accident and was never in the hospital. My family felt it was best to tell me when I was at home with them. My team leaders and project directors had been told of my dad's passing, but were instructed by my family not to tell me the news. I felt so confused and betrayed by everyone. I understood they had my best interest at heart, but finding out my dad had been dead for two days and no one had told me was just another dagger to my heart.

The next few days were packed full of funeral plans and family gatherings. The funeral came and went, things settled down, and the reality of the situation began to set in. As I thought through what had just happened, I began to feel as if I had been abandoned by God. I was a new Christian and didn't understand the concept of trials and challenges. All I knew was that I gave God my everything, and He had given me the greatest trial of my life in return.

I knew in that moment I had a decision to make. Was I going to continue to serve God or was I going to go back to my old way of life? As I lay on the floor, broken before God, He took me back to the moment I first met Him. That moment with Him was more real to me than any other in my life. I knew God was true, that He loved me, and even though I did not understand my circumstances, I would still follow him. After all, He had my heart. I was madly, deeply in love with Him and knew He would see me through. He was the only hope I had, so I made a declaration to the Lord that night, that no matter what the trial, pain, or hurt, we were in this thing together.

I had six months left of my senior year, which were some of the hardest months of my life, but hope was on the horizon. I had signed up to attend Teen Mania's Honor Academy, a program designed to cultivate and develop the leadership potential inside of you, while preparing you to impact the world for Christ. After my first experience with Teen Mania, I was a little terrified of what trials the enemy might throw my way, but I knew God was calling me there.

I graduated high school and spent my summer going on mission trips and volunteering at various youth camps before heading to the Teen Mania campus in Garden Valley, Texas. As I walked through the gates of Teen Mania, I felt hope fill my heart. I had spent my entire life feeling as if I were a prisoner to my parents' decisions, and now I was finally free and on my own.

I came to the Honor Academy a broken, insecure, and hurting young woman in desperate need of healing, and that is exactly what I got. As a first-year intern, I was not allowed to date, listen to secular music, or watch R-rated movies. I had spent the past year of my life with those same standards, so the rules were not a problem for me. It created an incredible atmosphere for growth.

That year was one of the hardest, but most rewarding years of my life. I developed amazing girlfriends, who are still my best friends today, received life-changing teaching, and had life-altering encounters with God. It seemed as if I was surrounded by the presence of God at all times and that was exactly what I needed. After 17 years of listening to my parents fight, 17 years of being disappointed and heart broken by their rejection and my own mistakes, and of being caught in my own insecurities, regrets, and un-forgiveness, I was finally free to become whole, to become the woman God wanted me to be.

That year I allowed God to be my Daddy, I allowed Him to restore my broken heart and piece me back together. I allowed Him to put dreams and desires back in my heart, to fill me with vision and passion for the world. I allowed Him to show me the woman I was to become who He was calling me to be, and yes, I allowed Him to show me the type of man I deserved one day.

My first year at the Honor Academy was coming to a close when I was hit with yet another life-altering trial. I called home one day to speak with my mother but her new, even more, dreadful, hideous boyfriend answered the phone. I was met with constant resistance when I asked to speak to my mom and I knew right away something was up. After ten minutes of questioning him, he finally told me my mom was in jail. "IN JAIL!" I shouted.

Now, my mom had made some pretty bad decisions in the past, but becoming a criminal was a bit extreme even for her. He would not give me any further details, so I phoned the police station to find out what charges had been brought against her. It turns out this boyfriend of hers had gotten her into a lot of trouble, and she spent the next five months in jail. In return for her taking the fall for his erratic behavior, he stole my mom's credit cards and jewelry and hit the road. I had a decision to make: stay a second year at the Honor Academy, which I knew God was calling me to, or move back home to take care of my mom's mess.

I had spent months warning my mom about this guy, but once again my advice fell on deaf ears. As usual, my mom chose a man over the well-being of her children and my heart ached for my mom. I knew she needed me more than ever before, but I knew I needed me, too. I needed to run after my life and the dreams God had for me. I could no longer allow my past to hold me back, so I made the decision to stay a second year and let my mom work out her own issues. Within a few months, my mom was released and began putting her life back together again, while I began my second year at Teen Mania.

I stayed for a program called Fellowship of the Burning Heart, a speaking mentorship facilitated by Ron Luce, the President and CEO of Teen Mania. I spent the next year reading books on speaking, character, and great men and women of faith. I also spoke twice a month before youth groups across the country, and after my second year at Teen Mania came to a close, I was hired on as a staff member with the ministry.

For the next year, I enjoyed a season of singleness. I lived with three amazing women of God. I spent endless nights of chocolate and chick flicks with the girls and developed some great friendships with my fellow brothers. I didn't think life could get any better and I was happy and content, but God had something up His sleeve. My life was about to take a dramatic turn for the better, and I had no idea what was coming!

My Prince Charming came into my life when I least expected it. He came over one day to use our computer, and that was the day my life changed forever.

CHAPTER THREE

A Divine Rescue:
Joel's Journey

"Before I shaped you in the womb, I knew all about you. Before you saw the light of day, I had holy plans for you …."

— Jeremiah 1:5

"You broke the bonds
And you loosed the chains
Carried the cross
Of my shame …
You know I believe it."

— U2, "I Still Haven't Found
What I'm Looking For"

W hile Casey wasn't raised in church, I grew up with a bit more expo-
sure to it. My mom and dad met at Bible College and got married.
Approximately a decade later, I was born in Redwood City,
California. I am the younger of two sons. I don't know all the details, but
it seems that my mom and dad's relationship was deteriorating around the
time I was born, because 14 months after my birth, they finalized their
divorce. My father left my mother for another woman who happened to be
one of my mother's "good" friends. He started a heavy regimen of hardcore
drugs and joined a biker gang.

My mother raised my older brother and me on her own. Like many
of you reading this book, if you were raised by a single-mother, you know
that most of the time money is scarce. In other words, you grow up poor.

If there's any "good" time to be poor, I think the best time would
be when you're a little kid because you don't really know you're poor. As a
child, you have inklings that something is different about you, but you
can't quite put your finger on it. I remember asking my mother questions
like, "How come nobody else drives around in a 1977, orange Ford Pinto,
with fake wood paneling on the sides, that backfires 10 times when you go
anywhere?" or "Why is the cheese so big?" As many of you know, welfare
cheese tastes fine, but it's big!

Also, as a poorer child, you begin to notice that you don't really
wear name brands. If you're lucky, maybe you wear pseudo-name brands or
"look-a-like" name brands. You know what I am talking about—instead of
your shorts having the adidas triple stripe running down them, it only has
one and half stripes. Or your shirt will say "Nike," but it's spelled N-I-K-Y.
It won't say, "Just Do It," but, rather, something close to it, like "You Can
Do it!" I also noticed there were name brands made just for poorer people.
They even sounded like they were made for poor people. Like Wal-Mart's
brand, "Faded Glory." I dejectedly asked, "Why's it got to be faded, huh?
Why can't it be new?"

We could never afford designer jeans either. The only "brand
name" jeans we could afford were called Bugle Boy. Bugle Boy? Really, the

marketers couldn't come up with a name better than that? What were they thinking? As a junior higher, I thought that they must have done this on purpose! I envisioned a bunch of marketing executives sitting around, in their pinstripe suits, smoking expensive cigars and saying, "Lets name our poor folk line of jeans something that will really keep them down. For our guys' line of jeans, let's name it something truly, quite-entirely, emasculating." I imagined one of them smiling an evil Grinch-like smile and saying, "Let's call it Bugle Boy," and the rest of them smiling and then in unison pronouncing, "Yes, let's call it Bugle Boy!" Then they would all laugh and congratulate each other for a job well done. How could they do this to me? I mean, who in the world would think that brand name would be appealing to junior highers? I was convinced it must have been a conspiracy.

How many junior high guys want to display a name brand on the back of their pants that invokes images of a prepubescent horn player? There are so many more cool (and much more manly) instruments than a Bugle. Come on, how many guys (or even girls, for that matter) aspire to play the bugle. Why didn't they at least call them something halfway more masculine like Drummer Dudes or Guitar Guys? Seriously, I just made those names up. It couldn't be that hard to come up with something better than Bugle Boy.

As well, have you ever noticed that "poor people" brands are always approximately two years behind what's in style? I remember when cargo pants were first coming into style. You know, the pants with multiple pockets down the legs. When it was time to buy some new school clothes, I had already prepared myself that Bugle Boy probably didn't make any of them yet. But to my surprise, they did have a pair of pants with a pocket on the side of one pant leg. I picked out my size and my mom purchased them. Excited about my pair of paints, with one leg-pocket on the side, I headed out for school.

What I quickly discovered was that there weren't really any other usable pockets anywhere else on the pants. So I was forced to put everything (my beanie, wallet, loose-change, love letters that I would write to myself so that people would think I had a girlfriend, etc.) into that one leg-pocket. When it was full, it looked like a huge growth hanging from the side of my leg. It also caused me to walk with a limp/swagger, which put me in a most unfortunate predicament when I had to walk past gang members in the hall at school. I could imagine them shouting at me, "What you claiming, Homes?" I wouldn't know what to say, so I'd probably reply something stupid like, "Umm … Bugle Boy?" Thinking I was trying to be sarcastic, they would probably chase me down, beat me up, and steal everything out of my pocket, except for the love letters I wrote to myself. Pragmatically, I decided not to wear those pants often. So goes life in a single-mom household.

When I was in 2nd grade, my mother left the welfare rolls and began working full time as a legal secretary. In the 5th grade, my mother met a man at work. She was excited at the prospects of companionship and receiving some much needed help in raising two boys. He also had two boys. I was excited about having some younger brothers. I had endured years of "brotherly" beat-downs generously lavished upon me by my older sibling. I thought I might have a few opportunities to bestow a similar brotherly blessing upon them. My mother eventual married their father and the beat-downs began, except they were anything but brotherly.

My stepbrothers and I never exchanged a single blow. Regrettably, the blows all came from my stepfather. During those years, clothes masked claret bruises. A house on five acres concealed my stepfather's cruel acts, which he executed under the influence of alcohol. It was fear that kept me from telling anyone about it and my mother from leaving him. He was so very cruel.

A Dark Night

Boom-thud! It was the sound of my stepfather's fist punching through sheet-rock walls. "I'm going to beat the hell out of that fagot!" His footsteps pounded down the hall toward the closed door of my bedroom. "He ain't good for anything but eating, sleeping." Boom-thud! His fist slammed through another wall. "He's a pussy, nothing but a Little Lord Fauntleroy!" (I didn't know who that was then, but I knew it must have been derogatory.)

"Come on, he's just a kid," my mother interjected.

"I'm going to throw his butt out his bedroom window!" my stepfather yelled. (My room was on the second floor!) My mother pleaded with him to go to bed, and finally, he did.

When my stepfather went to work the next morning, my mother woke me and my brother up, told us to get in the back of her 1984 blue Dodge hatchback colt, and we drove to her friend's house. Unbeknownst to my brother or me, my mother had been slowly taking our belongings to a storage unit over the last six months. She had also bought an Aerostar minivan and a small, pop-up, tent trailer. The van was a sparkly midnight blue with a three-foot wide, horizontal baby blue stripe running down both sides. A shiny metal silver ball poked out from under the back bumper. The trailer looked like a waist-high, white paper milk carton on wheels.

We packed our belongings into the Aerostar, hitched up the trailer and drove for hours. Long hours on the highway turned into winding mountain roads and dense forest. At dusk, we pulled into a campground and the camp manager directed us to our site. After removing the trailer from the van, my mother pulled out an "L" shaped crank from under the driver's seat, flipped open a small flap on the sidewall of the trailer, and slid the crank into the newly revealed hole. She twisted the crank clock-wise and the milk carton began to grow. First, the roof sprang up ten feet, chased by four yellow canvas walls. Then an aluminum door folded down from the roof and opened. The mustard-colored cube continued to transform, my mother still wildly twisting the crank. Out of its sides shot "king size" planks, which also popped up, growing to about half the size of the roof. In its final form, the trailer looked somewhat like a canvas Noah's Ark with plastic windows. We unpacked, settled in, and went to bed. I think it rained that night.

My stepfather went berserk when he found out we had left. He destroyed everything we left behind. My Great Grandmother's dining room chairs were smashed, the TV was thrown out of the second story window, and the crystal and china were shattered. He began searching for us and showed up at my mom's work looking for her. He called other family members inquiring about our location and when they refused to tell, spewed venomous threats. Honestly, no one knew where we were because my mom didn't tell anyone where we were heading. For now, as it rained, my mother, brother, and I took refuge in our ark, waiting for the storm to pass.

After some time, my mom got in contact with her friend from work. Her coworker said that her parents owned a cabin in the hills and were going to be vacationing there for a month. She said that her parents had offered their home to us while they were away. My mother accepted the offer. We packed everything back into the minivan, reverse-cranked the tent trailer, which miraculously folded itself back into its original milk-carton shape, latched the trailer back onto the silver hitch, and crept down the winding mountain road. We were heading for a place called Woodland. It sounded like a nice place, and it was, but unfortunately we wouldn't be there for long.

My mom enrolled my brother and me into school, where I surprisingly made friends really quickly. After a month, we moved into an apartment. Five months later, my mother thought she saw my stepfather's truck. His truck was pretty unique—charcoal black with a thin neon orange pinstripe. She told us that she didn't want to take any chances and, regretfully, that we really needed to move again. So we did. We packed up everything and took off. We were out on the road again, heading toward a town named Roseville. I wondered what it would be like transferring to another school months after it started, if I would make any new friends, and how long we would stay there.

At my new school, my circle of friends remained small, but my waistline continued to expand. In the 8th grade, I topped out at a whopping 250 pounds and was a magnet for ridicule. I was teased and called all the normal "fat" names like "hippo-hips," "thunder-thighs," and even "man-boobs." While my body was slower than most, the continual verbal assault of my classmates allowed me to perfect another skill—linguistic jujitsu.

Ninja quick "cut-downs," perfectly timed "comebacks," and guerrilla style "wise-cracks" were just a few weapons in my arsenal of tongue lashing techniques. It was the best defense I had and one I exercised regularly. I hated being overweight, but I was a teen trying to cope with my life continually falling apart. More painful than any blow to my body were the continuous beatings my heart underwent. I was a broken teenager with a broken heart.

Because I really didn't know how to cope with all that had happened to me, I numbed the pain by eating and food became my drug of choice. Drowning my sub-conscious sorrows in a super-sized soda and #1 combo-meal from McDonald's made me feel better, at least, while I was consuming them. While those around me recommended that I change what I ate, what I really needed was a changed heart.

A month before my freshman year of high school, my mother forced me to go to a church camp, which was the last thing I wanted to do. I told my mother I wasn't going. She said something like, "You don't have a choice. You're going, and that's final." The camp was a series of church services and competitive games. We played games from mud tug-o-war to eating competitions (e.g., what team member could eat a banana, drink a liter of soda, and spin around 50 times the fastest). Needless to say, the camp was a little bit of heaven and a little taste of hell. Looking back, I think it may have been purposely designed that way.

On the last night of camp, after a challenging message from the preacher, I came forward to give all of my life over to God. I felt a curious, heavenly warmth fill my body, and with it came peace, hope, and real joy. I lay on the floor for at least half an hour, basking in this wonderful feeling. I felt, at that time, that I was being touched by the hand of God and hearing His heavenly whispers. When I left the service, I felt that I had shed the skin of an old life, a life I would never return too. I felt alive and free from my past. I felt, in that moment, that nothing was impossible for me. I believed if God created the universe and I was fully given over to Him, nothing He created could hold me back. A part of me was brought back to life that night. It was like God reintroduced me back to myself— to the true me, the person I was to always become, the strong, good, and courageous me. It was a breathtaking night, a night I will never forget and one that changed the course of my life.

After the service, I got some really tasty nachos at the camp snack-shack. After wolfing them down, I felt drawn back to the chapel where I found scores of teenagers praying in the prayer room. The passion of their prayers enraptured me and I found myself joining them, praying to God with ardent abandon. We prayed for hours into the morning, all the while it felt as if the very Creator of the Universe was in the room with us. It was so energizing. I never guessed that praying could be such pure joy! It was finally a little taste of heaven in a life filled with so much hell. I was consumed with God.

When I got home, I tore down posters, broke CDs, and threw out everything that had hindered me from pursuing a life fully devoted to God. In my heart, I knew I had met God and had asked Him to walk with me and to live in me. He felt so close, and I didn't want that to end. I desired to remove any distraction that had kept me selfish, self-serving, and spiritually weak. I wanted to be fully alive. I wanted a life, with the Creator of Life, living in me. I had found real life, and I wasn't going to let any rapper, athlete, or celebrity distract me from it. So, they and their clutter went into the trash to make more space for God in my life. And that's exactly what happened—the more room I made for Him, the closer we became.

The amazing thing about God is that when you really find Him, you want more of Him. I would pray and read my Bible in my room and feel like there was no end to God's knowledge and personality. I loved reading about Jesus, God Among Us. He was the perfect man, brave but kind, loving but fierce, strong but gentle. He was so good to people, no matter their social status. Children felt like they could run into His arms, even while He was preaching (something you can't say about every preacher). He was eternal—eternally good, faithful, noble, brave, loving, fierce, strong, gentle, and merciful. I wanted to be just like Him.

For the first time, my life had real purpose. I felt my life on earth was God's gift to me, and I wanted the way I lived it to be my gift back to Him. I had resolved to live for Him bravely, no matter what other people thought or said about me, even if it was difficult or wasn't popular. Within a week of the camp, I made a commitment to read through the Bible, to set apart time to pray every day, and to abstain from dating until I felt the Lord leading me into a courtship (a relationship with the potential of marriage). I also made a decision to save my first kiss for the woman I would marry someday.

High School

My resolution to follow the Lord bravely was soon put to the test. My brother, who had already given his life to the Lord, challenged me to bring my Bible to school as a way of letting people know about my new commitment to follow Christ. I agreed to the challenge, but a month later, I was really nervous about what people would think about me when they saw me carrying a Bible around. I attended a California public high school and bringing a Bible to school was less than cool. It was an opportunity to be singled out and be made fun of, and it required that I leave the safety of "blending in with the crowd," something this freshman didn't want to do.

But I had made a commitment to follow Christ and had specifically promised my brother to bring my Bible to school, so the first day of my freshman year, I walked onto campus carrying my Bible—well, at least technically. I hid it underneath all the rest of my books. But as I walked toward my first period class, concealing my New King James, courage began to fill my heart. I thought to myself, "If I am really going to live for Jesus, I'm going to do it fearlessly."

I removed the hidden Bible from under my books and walked into my first period class. I sat down and put all my books underneath my desk, except my Bible, which I put right on top of my desk for everyone to see. A guy sitting next to me sarcastically asked, "Hey, like, what do you have a Bible for?" I tried to restrain from using the full force of my tongue-lashing arsenal by downgrading a completely sarcastic response to a semi-sarcastic one. I quasi-mockingly responded, "Hmm, a book? Well, maybe to read."

That seemed to silence the guy. And, actually, I didn't feel that bad about my sarcasm at that time. After all, I thought I was attempting to do what Saint James said was near impossible—tame the tongue (James 3:8). Reading the Bible was already having such an influence on me!

That was the beginning of taking a stand for Christ in high school. I started a Bible Club on campus in my sophomore year, pushing its charter through an opposing school administration. Our club held scores of prayer meetings around the flagpole, shared Christ with people on campus, and sponsored can and clothes drives for the homeless. It was scary and thrilling to stand up so boldly for Christ. I was made fun of and called names like Jesus Freak, Christian Man, and, my favorite, Holy Bowler (which I believe they called me because the church I attended was held in a former bowling alley).

I had a list of about 10 classmates I would pray for every night using Ephesians 1:16-24 as a guide. I called it my "Heaven's Hit List." I attended church almost everyday the doors were open. In the mornings before school I would pray for an hour with my pastor, youth pastor, and some other friends. Everyday seemed like a new adventure with God. It was not always easy standing for Christ, but the more I spoke up about Him and lived for Him, the more joy, peace, and life I felt surging inside of me.

I'll never forget one adventure God invited me into during my junior year. I was at youth service and my youth pastor gave a challenge to come forward and pray "if we wanted more of God in our lives." I came forward, got down on my knees, and began praying, "Lord, I do want more of you in my life. Please, fill me more with your Spirit." And then, after a few minutes of praying, it happened. I began to daydream. (I hate that. I still have to fight to not get distracted when I'm praying, or I start thinking about all sorts of things other than what I really want to pray about.)

Where was I again? Oh yeah, the daydream.

Like I said, after praying for a few minutes, my mind started to wander. I wish I could say that I was thinking about something really spiritual, but I was only thinking of gorditas from Taco Bell. Then, all of a sudden, in the middle of this delectable daydream, I began to see myself at high school standing on top of a bench preaching about Jesus in the middle of Senior Square. (Senior Square is a place on campus where most of the cool kids hung out. It was designated as a place where Seniors could eat lunch away from underclassmen.) At the time, I was a junior and really not supposed to be in there, but in my daydream I was preaching the Gospel and I thought, "Lord that's cool."

And then I felt like God said, "That's you, tomorrow at lunch time!"

Honestly, my first thought was, "God couldn't have said that," followed by another thought, "That doesn't make me feel very peaceful. It must have been Satan."

Then my normal line of questioning ensued upon "thinking" I heard God speak. Was that really God? Was that just my own mind? Why would God say that? Is this the Enemy pretending to be God? (I'll talk more about hearing the voice of God more clearly later on in the book.) All I knew was, whoever said it, it was a frightening proposition and one I wanted no part of. "Besides," I thought, "I can't do it because Juniors aren't allowed in Senior Square." The leading in my heart to preach there the next day, however, would not go away.

The next morning, I woke up and the first thought on my mind was, "Today's the day. You know you're supposed to do it." I didn't want to, but I felt that if I didn't I would be directly disobeying the Lord. I went to prayer in the morning and then to school. I told no one of what I felt I was supposed to do.

Lunchtime came along and I decided to eat lunch in the cafeteria, which is on the complete opposite side of the school from Senior Square. So, I'm sitting in the cafeteria at the table where a lot of Christians sat, and like a constant bass drum beating in between my temples, I felt like God was still saying, "Go now! Joel, you need to go now!"

So, me being the "obedient man of God" that I was, I didn't go to Senior Square. Instead, I went over to a table of girls and invited them to youth group. My thought was that maybe I could do something that was "good" and God would understand why I didn't do what He had asked me to do.

If you're thinking that I probably shouldn't have gone to talk to these girls, you're exactly right. I walked up to the table of girls and said, "Hey ladies! You should come to youth group with me. It'll be really cool!"

I'll never forget what happened next, because one of the girls stood up and said, "You don't tell me about no youth group! I've had eight years of religious school, baby!" Her neck began to move like she was a participant on the *Jerry Springer Show*. I thought at any moment one of his security guys was going to come out to break it up. Unfortunately, for me, they didn't. She kept going off on me. When she was done, she sat down and no one at the table said a word. I said the first thing that came into my mind, "It's not just about being religious or knowing about God, it's about really knowing Him. He changed my life."

The whole table of girls continued to ignore me and went back to eating whatever we ate in the cafeteria. (No one really ever knew exactly what we were eating, except that it always came with tater tots.)

You know that feeling that you get when you are being ignored, when you know other people can hear you, but they're totally pretending they can't hear you? A-N-G-E-R! I swear, in that moment, billows of smoke must have been steaming out of both ventricles of my heart. I left the table of disregarding girls. I was mad.

I put on my backpack and started pacing back and forth in the middle of the cafeteria. Then I busted through the double doors. There were eight hoodlums sitting on a bench right outside. They were all wearing creased Dickies and hooded sweatshirts. I walked over and said, "You guys need to know the Lord Jesus Christ! Romans 10:9 says if you confess with your mouth that Jesus Christ is Lord and believe in your heart that God was raised from the dead, you will be saved! Would you like to make Jesus the Lord of your life right now?"

They looked at me and surprisingly said, "Sure. Okay." All eight of us grabbed hands, and I led them in the Sinner's Prayer. (One of those "hoodlums" I still know. He went on to work at The Dream Center in Los Angeles for almost 10 years, working to get the homeless, prostitutes, and gangbangers off the streets.)

From there I headed to Senior Square, but now I had me a posse! Once in the Square, I hopped up on a bench and yelled out to the crowd of chattering students, "Come around, I've got something to say! Come around!"

Nobody moved, except for maybe three members of the chess team. Everyone else just stared. I began to share, "Jesus Christ has changed my life. He revolutionized my life. Most of us, if we're really honest, put on a mask everyday when we come to school. Some put on a hard face, others put on a happy face, pretending that everything is okay. But most of us are broken. Our hearts are broken inside. God is the only one who can fix it. He healed my heart. I know He can heal yours."

All of a sudden my vice principal came to the edge of the bench and barked, "All right, young man! Step down!"

I looked down at my vice-principal, then looked back at my peers, about 400 of them stood around listening, and I began to share again,

"God can change your life. He changed mine. He can heal any broken heart …."

My other vice-principal walked toward me and said, "Alright, step down!" I looked down at her, and what happened next I will never forget. Out of the crowd of 400 students, some began to shout, "Let him speak."

Then another yelled out, "Hey, let him speak!" followed by a roar of people screaming, "Let him speak! Let him speak! Let him speak!"

When I was done sharing, I stepped down from that bench and my vice-principal went off on me, yelling, "What gives you the right? What gives you the right?" As a teenager, I didn't know exactly what to say, so I replied, "The Mergens Case, held before the Supreme Court, gave us the Student Bill of Rights, which allows us to freely share our faith on campus."

With each word spoken, I noticed my vice-principal's face progressively turning deeper shades of red. He bellowed out, "What are you, some kind of Constitutional expert!?"

I looked over to my other vice-principal, and she said, "Why didn't you step down when we told you too?!" Tears began to run down my face as I replied, "Well, my friends are dying. They're on drugs. Some of them have committed suicide. Other friends were getting straight A's, but now they're flunking out of school. How can I stay silent when I've got the answer? His name is Jesus." They sent me to the principal's office.

I sat across the desk from my principal in his office. I was definitely intimidated. He said to me, "Young man you've got to promise me that you'll never do this again on my campus."

I looked him in the eyes and as respectfully as I could, replied, "Sir, I can't promise I won't do this again, but next time I do, I will let you know."

Somehow, I walked out of there without being suspended. Throughout that next week, I had the opportunity to lead 16 people to Jesus. I don't believe everyone is called to stand on a bench and preach the Gospel, but I know that God has a benchmark He desires all of us to attain. He is calling all of us to greater steps of faith and obedience for our sake and for those in the crowd crying out for someone to speak the truth.

After this, things began to change drastically for me at high school. A few months later, I ran against a very popular cheerleader for student body vice president, and I won. The next year, I emceed most of our pep rallies, was voted basketball homecoming king by the student body, and was voted as one of the Top Ten Seniors by the faculty and teachers. As an organizer on our class's graduation planning committee, I asked my principal if I could speak at graduation. Usually, only the Student Body President, Senior Class President, and Valedictorian get to speak, so I figured my principal would say no. Instead, he looked me in the eyes and quietly whispered, "Yes, but I don't want to know what you are going to say."

So, at my graduation, after the Student Body President, Senior Class President, and Valedictorian spoke. I got up to speak. I prayed over our class. I prayed God would bless us, guide us, and lead us in life. When I said, "Amen," surprisingly, I was met by a huge roar of screams and applause from my classmates, followed by an explosion of graduation caps thrust into the air.

After high school, I enrolled in a local community college part-time and spent the rest of my time pursuing rock stardom. *One Astray* was a three-piece "power-pop" band. We'd spend hours making music, traveling to shows (only to play a 30-minute set), and hanging out late into the night. It was the ultimate boys' club. We recorded one album, performed scores of times, and sounded absolutely horrible! These years were entirely entertaining—a young man's dream come true!

After *One Astray* disbanded, I accepted a roll at my church as the junior high youth director. I took the students to a youth conference called Acquire the Fire. I had attended the event before, during my senior year of high school. It had really impacted my life and I was hoping it would do the same for our church's students. It touched our teens' lives dramatically, but I think it affected mine even more. At the event, they shared about a one-year internship, called the Honor Academy, at the Teen Mania Ministries headquarters. I felt drawn to sign up for it, but the internship was based in Texas. So for this bread-and-born Californian guy, I had no desire to leave paradise for, what I thought, was a desert prairie. But the year looked so exciting, chock-full of adventure—going overseas, trekking Pikes Peak, etc. At the same time, every adventure was focused on building character, leadership and spiritual development. I felt so drawn to go. I prayed about it throughout the next week. I would have to take a year break from college, stop volunteering as a youth director (which I loved), and move to Texas, away from my family and friends. It was a big step for me, and I had to be sure the Lord wanted me there. I didn't know if I was too old, at age 21, because I knew that most of the attendees were 18 and coming straight out of high school.

Looking back now it seems a little silly, but I really thought I was too old. I thought I probably needed to settle down and finish college, especially since I had come to the realization that I most likely wasn't going to be a rock star. I was wrestling with what I should do when the Holy Spirit, thankfully, interrupted my professor's *A River Runs Through It* lecture. He spoke so clearly, "Will you regret not going at age 21, when your 25?" Instantly, my decision became crystal clear. "Yes," I thought to myself, "I will genuinely regret not going." So, six months later, I packed almost everything I owned into a few suitcases and headed for Texas. I didn't know it then, but this choice would be one of the most life-altering decisions of my life.

To recount all the amazing adventures I had at the Honor Academy, traveling across the country and around the world, would take volumes to recount. All I will say is that those were some of the best years of my life. I grew as a servant, a leader, and a communicator. I drew closer to God and gained a lot of clarity about His purpose and plan for my life.

The next year, Ron Luce, the President of Teen Mania Ministries, offered 30 Honor Academy interns an opportunity to stay for a speaking internship. Eight of us chose to participate. We called ourselves The Fellowship of the Burning Heart. In order to continue in the fellowship, you had to find at least two places to speak at every month. We recorded our messages and exchanged recordings with other members in the Fellowship. We then critiqued each other's messages and gave written constructive comments to each other. We also had to critique a recording of a professional speaker or preacher.

Every month, Ron chose three books for us to read that had impacted his life or improved his communication. We were required to read and write a report on each of them. I learned a lot that year, got some great practice speaking, and got to know Ron Luce a lot better. Before the year was over, he invited me to come speak with him at an event in Washington D.C. Of course, I agreed. That day, I preached my heart out in front of half a million of my peers, as we all fasted and prayed for God to move powerfully in our country.

After a year of developing our speaking skills, a group of five of us, inspired by the Student Volunteer Movement (an American movement that eventually saw over 20,000 college students head overseas to preach the gospel to the nations), desired to inspire as many people as possible to get tangibly involved in completing the Great Commission. We called ourselves Servants of the Call. We headed out on the road speaking to any group who would listen. For the next two years, I spoke six times a week, three weeks a month, for almost ten months out of the year. And somehow, I was able to keep up with 3 or 4 correspondence college courses each semester. I then spent the two months of summer on the mission field.

I couldn't get enough of reaching out to the hurting and broken around the world and inspiring Christians to make a difference around the globe. During that time, I nearly lived in the 15-passenger van we traveled in and slept on hundreds of floors across America. In those two years, I spoke before almost 400 different congregations. During this time, I fell in love with the people of the United States. In every state, there are kind, generous, and gracious people. We were hosted by hundreds of families who, though they had never met us before, warmly welcomed us into their homes and treated us like family.

Halfway through my first tour with Servants of the Call, I received a call from Ron Luce. He asked me if I wanted to co-host an Acquire the Fire event with him. I excitedly agreed to do it. Three weeks later, at the age of 24, I led over 10,000 teenagers through a weekend of incredible ministry. When I first stepped onto the stage, I was so nervous my legs were shaking. But, thankfully, after I told a few jokes and the audience actually responded in laughter, I relaxed. I felt at peace, preached from the deepest, truest place in my heart, and saw hundreds of teens come to know the Lord.

I was very busy during this season of my life and I really didn't have time for a girlfriend. Honestly, being single was okay with me. It was my season of singleness. My life was one great adventure after another with God. I was traveling around the nation and the world, sharing about God and helping people. Everyday, I met new people who were helping others in their communities. I got to worship with nearly every Christian denomination. I felt God so close to me all during that time. It was a Bible-believing bachelor's paradise.

Now, if you're wondering right now, as some did then, yes, I did like girls. So, why didn't I date? First, I was pretty busy, as I mentioned. Second, I don't think I was ready. I had a lot of maturing to do and my heart still needed a lot of healing. Third, I hadn't come across a young lady who struck me as someone I would want to marry. Don't get me wrong, I met some great, godly, beautiful, gorgeous women, but the best way to describe it is that none of them fit what my heart was looking for. I knew there was a soul mate for me, and I knew whenever He wanted, God, the Great Shepherd, could lead even this sometimes-nearsighted sheep to her.

Then one day in prayer I felt I heard the Lord say, "I'm going to get you ready for a relationship." I took notice. What was going to happen?

After this prompting, I began reading books on courtship and marriage to help get me at least a little more prepared for this ensuing "relationship." I was excited about it, but didn't see any potential gals I was interested in. I went over to Ron's office for a meeting, during which he asked me, "So, are you interested in anyone?"

I said, "Ron, I am open to a relationship, but I haven't really found anyone I'm quite captured by."

He inquiringly said, "Really?"

I explained, "I hung out with a girl I was kind of interested in, but after hanging out for a bit, I'm definitely not interested anymore."

What Ron asked next shocked me, "Have you ever met Casey, my assistant?" I had never heard Ron try to set anyone up before. Ron's wife, Katie, is more than happy to help in this way, but Ron? Never.

I said, "I know Casey and talked to her briefly one time, but besides that, no."

He said, "Casey is the kind of girl I would want my son to marry." Errk! Slam on the brakes for one second! First, I respect Ron deeply for many reasons. I especially respect his family relationship. His wife Katie is madly in love with him and is full of spunk and life, and he loves their three kids and they adore him. So when Ron said this to me, I took it to heart.

I said, "Well, I guess I'll have to go get to know her then." A week later, I was over at a friend's apartment hanging out and by pure happenstance I found out that Casey lived in the same apartment complex. I thought, "This is as good of a time to meet her as any."

I came up with some lame excuse, like needing to use her computer, and then made my way to her and her roommates' apartment. That was the first time I hung out with Casey, and let's just say, after that I was very interested in hanging out again.

CHAPTER FOUR

THE BACHELOR
(FOR MEN ~~ONLY~~) *and women!*

"The Man named the cattle, named the birds of the air, named the wild animals; but he didn't find a suitable companion."

— Genesis 2:20

"And in the end, it's not the years in your life that count. It's the life in your years."

— Abraham Lincoln

"He's learned it all from God-of-the-Angel-Armies, who knows everything about when and how and where."

— Isaiah 28:29

A dam was the ultimate bachelor. He was the most wealthy, powerful, and eligible individual on the planet. The world was his. He was a scientific explorer, namely, a taxonomist. He was fully engaged in naming and classifying millions of species of insects, fish, birds, mammals, and reptiles (Genesis 2:19-20). I can only imagine the adventures he must have had. All the earth's untouched land and sea was his to explore first. If humanity had the records of his ventures, we would find Adam listed in the records of the greatest adventurers of all time—next to the likes of Louis & Clark, Sir Edmond Hillary, and Neil Armstrong. Adam was made for exploration and charged to bring order to a wild, untamed earth (Genesis 1:26-28). He was young, courageous, and was a chip off the old eternal block, God's Pride-and-Joy (Genesis 1:27).

Adam and God were inseparable. God was his Dad, his Mentor, and his Friend. They were perfect for each other—an ideal dad and a fault-less son. I'm sure they were just crazy about each other! Nothing ever came between them or separated them then. Their hearts were close. They were two of a kind—a dynamic duo—best friends, like father, like son (Luke 3:38).

Life was almost perfect for this bachelor, except he was having one major issue—finding a girlfriend. (No matter how many times he submitted his compatibility criteria to eHarmony, not a single match for him was found.) Sadly, Adam couldn't get a date if his life depended on it. It wasn't because of any glaring social inadequacy though, but because, literally, there was no one else. It was a womanless-world. Before the Divine Matchmaker ever brought a woman into Adam's life, He arranged for Adam to have a season of singleness.

I loved being a bachelor, that is, before Casey came along. My single buddies and I adopted an acronym that helped describe our outlook on life. We were BTR (Bachelors to the Rapture) and we wore those letters like a badge of honor.

Hey ladies, this is Casey. Have you ever been mystified by the male mind? Have you ever encountered a guy whose words communicate one thing, but his body language says something completely different? This chapter will give you greater insight into how men see the world and see you! The chapter was written for men, by a man (Joel). And inside of the following pages you will not only learn more about how men think and what they desire, but unlock some key principles you'll need-if you're going to successfully venture down the road of romance with one of them. So put on your thinking caps and get ready to engage the left side of your brain (the reasoning side) as we prepare to unlock some of the mystery surrounding the male mind.

The single life was good, and the boys and I were determined to live life to the fullest. We had numerous females in our circle of friends, but none of us wanted to settle down with any of them. The soundtrack to our life then was the David Byrne's version of *Don't Fence Me In*:

> Oh, give me land, lots of land, under starry skies above
> Don't fence me in!
> Let me ride through the wide-open country that I love
> Don't fence me in
> Let me be myself in the evening breeze
> Listen to the murmur of the cottonwood trees
> Send me off forever, but I ask you please
> Don't Fence me in

We were wild stallions who didn't want to be saddled, lassoed, or tied down. Our hearts craved wide-open spaces. Every summer, we heard the call of the wild and answered it, traveling to some far-off region of the globe. I'll never forget those days, navigating down the Amazon River, living in a hut in the Darien Jungle in Panama, participating in Maori Hangi feasts and ceremonies in New Zealand, playing music throughout the war torn city of Beirut, trekking to the top of Yosemite's Half Dome and Pike's Peak in Colorado, walking the streets of Hanoi, riding elephants through the jungle of Change Mia, and overseeing the remodeling of a playground at an orphanage in Change Rai, Thailand.

I felt like God and I were inseparable. God was my Dad, Counselor, and Friend. I was so crazy about Him and sensed He felt the same about me. Our hearts were so close. We were two of a kind—a dynamic duo— best friends! He was my Father. I was His son. Before the Divine Matchmaker ever brought Casey into my life, He arranged for me to have a season of singleness, which may have been the most important period in my life.

As I mentioned, it was a season of much international exploration, but it was also a time of vast internal exploration. It was my time to figure out who I was, what I wanted, and where I was going. I broke out of a thousand mental cages, breaking free from the expectations of my friends, family, and church family to follow God with a brave heart wherever He would lead.

I was on a quest for truth. I hit the gym, hit the books, and even got some good hits in on my older brother (in the boxing ring, where not one of his knock-out blows even grazed me). I developed a love for playing basketball, lifting weights, and running. I delved into a lot of the classics, fell in love with C.S. Lewis's works (beyond the ones where Aslan shows up), graduated from college, and spent blissful hours praying, journaling, and studying God's Word.

This was also a time of restoration and growing whole. It seemed God was bent on healing my heart from the many wounds inflicted during my less-than-perfect upbringing. He started with the deepest wound first—the trauma that had twisted my perception of myself, life, and most unfortunately, God. He came to heal my fatherlessness. The abandonment of my father and the abuse of my stepfather had left me feeling unwanted, unloved, and alone. Of course, I couldn't see that then. All I knew was that there was an aching in my soul and whatever I tried to medicate the pain with wore off, or caused further complications. My heart had found some much-needed relief when I had given my life over to God, but my soul, under the surface, was still trying to escape the pain.

I'll never forget the night at a camp when I was hanging out in the back of the chapel, singing along with the worship musicians. The camp service had been dismissed, but there were about five people still praying. As I was singing songs to God, I felt this strong prompting to go forward to the steps up front and get down on my knees and pray. I didn't know why. I had come forward the night before to repent of my sins and ask for God's grace to change. I didn't feel there was anything separating me from God, yet I felt drawn to go forward. I walked up front, got down on my knees, and began to pray. I was asking the Lord if there was anything I needed to change or do or stop doing when I heard these words race through my mind, "Joel, I want to be your Daddy."

Tears began rolling down my cheeks. Thoughts of my dad leaving my mom and the years of abuse I endured by my stepfather flooded my mind. Hearing the word "Daddy" brought me back to a place I hadn't visited for years. The word spoke directly to my orphaned heart, exposing a very tender place of need.

As a child, I desperately desired a dad. Deep down, I hoped a strong, fathering man would want to be a part of my life. What boy doesn't want a father who will teach him how to play sports, cheer him on from the stands, teach him how to build things, show him how to hunt or camp, and think you are the greatest son ever? I always hoped someone like that would come along, but he never did. At some point in my childhood, I shut down the part of my heart that desired to be the much-loved child of a father. Holding on to the hope was just too painful.

When my stepfather first came into my life, my heart hoped he might be the dad I had always dreamed of, but when the abuse began, I locked that part of my heart shut and threw away the key. I had a dad— he walked away. I had a stepfather—he abused me. What I needed was a daddy, someone who was strong enough, tender enough, concerned enough, wise enough, wealthy enough, patient enough, and engaged enough to lead me out of the black hole in my heart and then through this life.

Have you ever been surrounded by people, but still felt lonely? That describes how I felt pretty much all the time during this period. Even with all the loving people in my life, I felt I was on my own. It's a heavy burden to be a boy and feel like you have to figure out what it means to be a man all by yourself. Even though my mom showered me with loving words like "I love you, I am proud of you, you are my son, and no one on this planet could replace you," I still desperately needed to hear those words from a father. The orphan inside my heart needed to hear, "I want to be your Daddy."

Finally, hearing those words that night set this prisoner free. After many sobs and tears, I accepted God's offer. I don't know exactly everything that happened in my heart then, but I do know that for the first time in my life, I felt like I wasn't on my own anymore. The way I viewed life rapidly began to change.

Before, I had envisioned my heavenly Father to be like my earthly fathers. I knew God accepted me, but I felt like He mostly tolerated me. I felt God wasn't close to me. I often felt like I had to walk on eggshells with God, like I did with my stepfather, just hoping I wouldn't make a mistake. I thought God would reject me unless I was perfectly obedient.

When I realized God desired to lovingly father me, I opened the door for Him to make my heart whole. During my season of singleness, God started the process of repairing my heart, and step-by-step, year-by-year, He continues to pick up the pieces of my shattered childhood, melding the shards back in their proper places and restoring my soul. He's making all things new (Revelations 21:5).

In the same way He did with my heart, God wants to make your heart new and heal its wounds. Actually, this is the very reason that Jesus came. He came to *"heal the heartbroken, announce freedom to all captives, pardon all prisoners"* (Isaiah 61:1). This is why the season of singleness is so important. It is a time of hanging out with God and focusing on Him while He transforms you.

Before we can ever think of joining our heart with another person in marriage, we have to be sure our heart is whole. In the arithmetic of love, two halves of a heart don't make a whole. It takes two whole hearts to make a whole relationship. Allow God during this season to make your heart whole. As Ephesians 1:4 says, *"Long before He laid down earth's foundations, He had us in mind, had settled on us as the focus of His love, to be made whole and holy by His love."*

Throughout my season of singleness, the Lord helped me become more whole. He helped me to work hard, yet trust Him to be my Provider. He assisted me in breaking free of a poverty mentality so I could dream big. God helped me stop looking to food as a source of comfort. He set me free from a habit of looking to women for affirmation, encouragement, and approval. He taught me to look to Him. He set me free from so many lies I believed about myself!

Every human soul is broken by sin and will always need repair, but before you ever think about starting a relationship, you must have a certain level of wholeness. Let me give you an example. There's a certain level of wholeness your car has to have before a father will allow you to drive his daughter around on a date. He will probably allow you to pick her up in a car that doesn't have a stereo, has a scratch in the paint job, or a rip in the backseat interior. This car, though not perfect, is at least mechanically whole enough to get his daughter to wherever you're going and back home by 9 p.m. sharp.

But you better not even think about showing up to his house without headlights, missing a tire, or without a steering wheel. Your car may have a brand new paint job, leather seats, and furry dice hanging from the rear-view mirror, but if the car is not to a certain level of wholeness, you're not going anywhere with his daughter (at least not with his blessing, anyway).

That's why our season of singleness is so essential for every man. It's a time to hang out with Dad while He helps you get your car running and teaches you how to keep it that way. So, take some time with your heavenly Dad, open up the hood of your heart and let Him look around.

A Few Maintenance Tips:

"And let me live whole and holy, soul and body, so I can always walk with my head held high." —Psalm 119:80

What a shame it would be if you and your father spent all that time fixing your car and making it whole, but because you didn't know how to maintain it you had to keep repairing the same things over and over again. Instead of investing your time, money, and energy into putting in a new stereo or getting a new paint job, you had to keep repairing the same old stuff.

Though your Dad never gets tired of hanging out with you in the shop, that's not His only desire. Your Father also wants you to experience the joy of living life out on the road! Learning how to maintain your heart can save you from hours, years, or potentially a lifetime of heartaches.

Ninety-five percent of learning how to maintain your heart is learning how to walk in holiness. For years I didn't know what in the world "holiness" meant! It only showed up in my vocabulary in phrases such as "Holy Smokes!" and the like. I had also heard the word used to negatively describe someone who thought they were superior to others (e.g., "Don't give me that holier-than-thou attitude!").

As I've learned what holiness really means, it has become one of my favorite words. Eugene H. Peterson, translator of the Message Bible, describes holiness as "the most attractive quality, the most intense experience we ever get of sheer life—authentic, firsthand living, not life looked at and enjoyed from a distance. We find ourselves in on the operations of God himself, not talking about them or reading about them. Holiness is a furnace that transforms the men and women who enter into it. 'Holy, Holy, Holy' is not needlepoint. It is the banner of a revolution, the revolution."

Living a holy life means choosing to operate your life in accordance with how God designed you to live. It's setting your life apart to be all God created you to be. Holiness is a choice to respect the amazing creation you are and treating yourself as that amazing creation. Life is a gift from God, and living holy makes your life a gift back to God. Holiness is a choice to respect yourself and the way your Creator made you. Holiness means living the way God made you to operate.

When you choose to live a holy life, you keep yourself from wasting months and years of having to repair a broken heart. A huge purpose of your season of singleness is allowing God to make you whole. You can only become whole if you allow God to make you holy, and the more holy you become, the more whole God can make you.

Wholeness and holiness are necessary to become all God desires you to be. Wholeness and holiness are like the legs of your heart. Without both of them it is impossible to run the race God has determined you to run—to live the life He wants you to live!

Before we head out on the road of romance, we have to set apart some time to visit the repair shop. We need to repair the brokenness and learn how to operate our lives as God designed them so that we can avoid breaking down. In the repair shop, God is going to give you the owner's manual. You must read it to understand how you were made to operate.

Read the Owner's Manual

"Every part of Scripture is God-breathed and useful one way or another—showing us truth, exposing our rebellion, correcting our mistakes, training us to live God's way." —II Timothy 3:16

An owner's manual tells you all you need to know about your car. The manual gives detailed instructions concerning every aspect of your vehicle. When I was a teenager, I never read or even referenced the owner's manual on any of my cars. I won't go into detail, but I blew the engines on both my first and second car. If I had taken five minutes to consult the owner's manual, I would have saved myself a lot of time, energy, and thousands of dollars in repairs.

Like an owner's manual, the Bible tells us everything we need to know about the human machine. Psalm 119:124 calls the Scripture the *"textbook on life."*

The Bible also gives detailed instructions on how we are to live and it gives insight on how we were designed to operate so that we don't use our hearts and bodies in a way that lands us in the repair shop. Some people say that the Bible is just a bunch of old rules to keep people from having fun and living free. Now it's true that the Bible does have rules (What instruction manual doesn't?), but the rules are there not to stop you from having fun but to keep you from breaking down. This is true concerning our body, spirit, and heart. Here's a sample scenario:

> The owner's manual for Jim Bob's car instructs him to use unleaded fuel only. Jim Bob thinks his owner's manual is being really mean and just wants to stop him from having a little fun. He decides to ignore the manual's instructions and pumps jet fuel into his tank in hopes it will make him go really fast. Jim Bob's vehicle does in fact go really fast, but unfortunately it is also engulfed in flames. Jim Bob and his car are now in need of major repair.

If you've neglected to follow the instructions in your Owner's Manual and your life is in need of major repair, all is not lost. Learn from your mistakes, open up your Bible, and follow the instructions. Like the Psalmist discovered, *"My troubles turned out all for the best—they forced me to learn from your textbook"* (Psalm 119:71).

CLEAN THE OUTSIDE OF THE GLASS

"Reverently honor an older woman as you would your mother, and the younger women as sisters." —I Timothy 5:2

If you can't see clearly, you won't be able to navigate properly. Most of us need a major scrubbing when it comes to how we view women. This is the first thing that we must do in order to have any hope of successfully navigating the road of romance in the future.

Paul explained how a godly young man should view girls. He said, *"Reverently honor younger women as sisters"* (I Timothy 5:2). Paul uses the analogy of seeing all girls as sisters. Wow, how much would our lives change if we actually took this to heart? What if guys didn't view young ladies as potential girlfriends, but saw them as sisters instead?

This is totally opposite of what we see on TV, the movies, and the Internet. Women are mainly portrayed as sex objects. If you have a sister, you may think she's cute-in-a-sisterly-way (most brother's don't even go that far), but you would never think of her as a sex object. And if some guy tried to treat your sister as one, you would probably feel it proper to bestow the blessing of a brotherly beat-down upon him.

There will be a day when the Divine Matchmaker will lead you to the right girl who will be your wife, your lover, and your best friend. She will be your Eve. It will be "very good," but until that happens, reverently honor older women as your mothers and young ladies as you sisters.

Remember, God is the Father of all of us. Not only is He your Dad helping you to repair your heart in the shop, but He is also the Father of the girl you're going to pick up on a date. As your Dad, God wants to teach you how to nobly win the heart of your dream-girl, but He is also that dream-girl's Father.

You do NOT want to mess around with one of God's daughters. I hear He's pretty protective.

CLEAN THE INSIDE OF THE GLASS

"Anyone who even looks at a woman with lust in his eye has already committed adultery with her in his heart." —Matthew 5:28

How we view a woman in our heart is of great importance to God. Our hearts lead our bodies. Jesus came not just to make our actions good, but to make our hearts good as well. He wants our thoughts, wishes, and desires to be holy and wholly good. If you let Him, He will do just that.

What I think is fascinating is that Jesus doesn't want to do this alone. He wants us to join Him in the process. After saying anyone who looks lustfully at a woman has committed adultery, Jesus says, *"So if your eye—even if it is your good eye—causes you to lust, gouge it out and throw it away. It is better for you to lose one part of your body than for your whole body to be thrown into hell. And if your hand—even if it is your stronger hand— causes you to sin, cut it off and throw it away. It is better for you to lose one part of your body than for your whole body to be thrown into hell"* (Matthew 5:29-30 NLV).

Now, we live in an age where the majority of advertisements use sex to sell. A lot of the ads are actually designed to provoke you to lust after a woman. I'm not even talking about the Internet where pornography runs rampant. We know God desires us to look at ladies older than us as mothers and ladies around our age or younger as sisters, but media and advertising make it very difficult to keep this perspective. (For more information on how media and advertising affects us, I recommend reading

Emerge, a book I co-wrote with Lisa Dunne. It is eye opening, to say the least! See www.thedivinematchmaker.com to order.)

So, we have to join into Christ's work of making our hearts whole and holy. Jesus recommends that if your eye or your hand is causing you to sin, you should cut them out or off. Wow and ouch! He said it would be better to do that than to burn in hell. Jesus doesn't sugarcoat things, that's for sure. But before you go cutting off one of your appendages, let's think of some other things you could cut off instead.

If you can't stop looking at pornography online, why don't you cut off using the Internet when you're alone in your bedroom? If you've been watching shows or DVDs that provoke you to lust, then sever your TV and DVD player from your bedroom and choose not to watch any media that does this. If your friends are all about sex and girls, then they can't be your best friends anymore. As the old adage goes, "You can't soar with eagles if you're running with turkeys."

I cut off a lot of things as a teenager, even choosing to fast media all together for periods of time. Sometimes, I just needed a break from it all and would only listen to music that lined up with what the Bible taught or I'd listen to a lot of sermons. I even cut the amount of time I played video games. (That was hard!)

I also chose not to look at girls in a sexual way or to let my mind fantasize about them. When I found my mind wondering, I would repent (turn to God) and ask God to help me. If I saw some really hot girl, I was determined not to look twice at her body. When I talked to girls, I always looked them in the eyes. I tried to view and treat girls around my age as sisters and older women as mothers.

Was I perfect at it? No way. But every time I looked at a girl lustfully, I turned to God, asked Him to forgive me, and chose to focus on viewing women purely, as sisters. In II Corinthians 10:5 (NIV) the Bible describes this as "*taking captive every thought to make it obedient to Christ.*" I like how the Message version says it: "*We use our powerful God—tools for smashing warped philosophies, tearing down barriers erected against the truth of God, fitting every loose thought and emotion and impulse into the structure of life shaped by Christ.*"

Any of our own warped philosophies, loose emotions, and impulses must be surrendered to Christ in exchange for what Christ says life should be like. His higher thoughts must replace our lower ones.

My youth pastor always told me that whatever you choose to feed in your life will grow strong. He said that inside of each of us is a war to choose right or wrong. If you choose to feed the part of you that wants to do wrong, it will win every time. If you choose to feed the part of you that wants to do right, then you will do right. He said that if you don't let anything evil into your heart, then it's less likely that evil will come out.

Jesus wants to make you whole and holy, but He doesn't want to do it alone. What do you feel you need to cut out of your life to keep your heart from lusting? Take a moment right now and write them out below:

The Father is serious about how we view His daughters. Lust is a sin and sin separates us from God, which is the last thing God wants. So, if you need God to help you change your view of how you see women, turn to God, ask Him to heal your heart and to make you whole, and then cut out everything that *"causes you to sin."*

I've prayed this prayer many times:

Dear Father, forgive me for looking at your daughters lustfully. I desperately want to change. I know I cannot do it on my own. I need your help. Come and heal my heart and make me holy. I choose to cast down every thought that is not in line with your thoughts and commands. Change my heart and set me free to look upon your daughters purely, as sisters. In Jesus' name, amen.

Stay In Between the Lines

While most guys are usually attracted to girls by how they look, what attracts girls to guys is a little more complex. Girls are attracted to good-looking guys, but what they really desire is a guy who emotionally connects with their heart. Guys, the battle we face to look at females purely is similar to the battle they face with their emotions. Girl's love to be emotionally connected. They love to talk and they love to talk about issues of the heart. Many girls today did not grow up with a father who was present (physically or emotionally) in the home, so they are starving for a heart-to-heart connection with a guy.

As a teen, I was completely unaware of this. I had a number of young ladies I was friends with and I often shared deeper things with them. I never specifically talked about anything romantic or hinted that I had romantic intentions, but the deep conversation and time we shared together communicated just that!

I know for a lot of guys this comes as a shock, but it's so true! Just as it is difficult to keep your mind from fantasizing impurely about a hot girl wearing revealing clothing, so it is difficult for a young lady to keep her mind and emotions from fantasizing about what a lifetime spent together with you would be like when you spend hours of time talking heart-to-heart and connecting emotionally with her.

You might not mean it, but you are making life difficult for them! For most ladies, time equals relationship. The more time talking together and hanging out, the harder it will be for her to guard her emotions and the more emotionally attracted she will be to you.

Not long ago, I was eating out with some friends of mine. One of the guys was dating a girl, so the other married guys at the table began asking him some questions about their relationship. The young guy didn't know where the relationship was going; he was just enjoying their long heartfelt talks. One of the married guys at the table (we'll call him, John) cautioned the guy on getting too emotionally involved with her if he wasn't sure where God was leading him in the relationship. John was in his 30s when he got married and was still a virgin.

Now, I have to call a time-out here. I want to explain a little about John because I know some of you are already thinking this guy must be the *40-Year Old Virgin* incarnate. John is nothing like the Steve Carell character. John is a rock star. No, really, he is. He's been nominated for multiple Grammy's and has traveled with the biggest bands in the music industry.

Not only does he know how to rock, but he's really intelligent as well. He has a M.A. degree in English. In addition, he's a good-looking guy who was willing to wait to have sex until he got married to the woman God had for him.

Leading up to his wedding, John was thinking what a miracle it was that he had remained physically pure for all those years. He thanked God for it. While he was contemplating this, John said he felt like the Lord lovingly said, "Yes, while you remained a physical virgin, you did not stay an emotional virgin."

Ouch! John had remained physically pure, but he had gotten emotionally involved, had led many girls on, and broken a few hearts. Though they weren't physical affairs, they were emotional affairs. John repented and asked the Lord, and the woman he was about marry, to forgive him for his past mistakes. John was glad God pointed this out to him. He could now turn to God and ask Christ to change his heart. John was also glad because he didn't want to carry this habit into his marriage.

Most of us have heard that we need to guard our physical purity, but we must also guard our emotional purity. Proverbs 4:23 (NLV) says, *"Above all else, guard your heart, for it affects everything you do."*

Now that you are equipped with this information, guys, we have a choice to make. Will we take advantage of our sister's struggle or will we choose to be real Christian brothers and protect our sisters the best we can? Just like it's good for girls to be conscious of their brothers' temptations by dressing modestly, it's good for guys to be conscious of their sisters' temptations by being emotionally modest.

As a general rule, avoid spending time alone with them often or always hanging out with them if you're in a group or allowing your conversations to go too deep. I want to stress that this isn't a rigid rule. It shouldn't create weirdness between you and your friends of the opposite gender. These are just some wise guidelines to help protect your sisters' hearts and help keep you from communicating, in girl-language, something you as a guy might have no clue you are saying. This is a skill that you will use the rest of your life, whether you marry or not.

When you are married to your dream girl, you would never want to communicate, unknowingly, to another woman that you're interested in her. Practicing these skills now will set you up for long-term success with your future bride. The season of singleness is the time to develop and practice physical and emotional purity.

GPS (ARE We THERE YET?)

Not only is your season of singleness a time to get to know God better, it's also a time to obtain greater direction from God. It's a season to gain more clarity on who you are supposed to be, what you are supposed to do, and where He wants you to do it. It's a time to find vision. God wants to lead you into all He has planned for you. He knows you won't be able to lead someone else if you don't know where you are going. Ask God, and He will direct you. James 1:5 says, *"If you don't know what you're doing, pray to the Father. He loves to help. You'll get His help, and won't be condescended to when you ask for it."*

Adam had direction from God and a job before God brought Eve into his life. These are two things all of us guys should have before we even think about pursuing a serious relationship. We must be able to provide. Proverbs 24:27 (NLV) says, *"Develop your business first before building your house."*

Take the time to figure out what you love to do and get skilled in it. For many of you, this means going to college, and for others, it means becoming skilled in a trade. Either way, you should have a sense of what career you want to pursue and begin moving in that direction so you can someday *"build your house"* and support your lady.

Having a firm grasp of God leading you in life is essential. Just like it's a good idea to know where you are going before you take a girl on a date, so it's a good idea to know where you are going in life before you start dating.

The ultimate goal of a romantic relationship is marriage, but marriage is not the ultimate goal of life. Life's ultimate goal is to be close to God. Adam walked and talked with God. They were dear allies and devoted friends. Adam was not primarily created for Eve; Adam was made for God. God wanted to hang out with Adam and have a close father-son relationship. Only after this relationship was tightly solidified did God bring Eve into Adam's life.

First things first, whether you ever get married or not, you must get close to God. If you don't, you miss the whole point of life, miss the whole purpose of why you were created, and most unfortunately miss out on eternal life. John 17:3 (NLV) says, *"And this is the way to have eternal life— to know You, the only true God, and Jesus Christ, the one You sent to earth."* God is pure life and the only way to have a life and share that life with another is to wholeheartedly center our lives around God. Romans 8:6 says, *"Attention to God leads us out into the open, into a spacious, free life."*

If you've been far from God, now is the time to draw close. James 4:8 says, *"Draw close to God and He will draw close to you."* He sent His son to die as a sacrifice for our sin. All our rebellion against Him and running away from Him has been forgiven. You just have to turn to God and He'll heal you (Matthew 13:15). If you have never fully given your life over to God, or if you and God have drifted apart in your relationship, turn to God and He will forgive you, embrace you, and heal you.

If you are ready to turn to your heavenly Dad, take some time now and pray. I have included the following prayer, so feel free to use it as a guide:

> Father, I turn to You. I give my life to You. You are eternal life and I want Your life to live in me. I give You all of me. I believe Jesus paid the price for my sins through His crucifixion and was resurrected again. There is nothing separating me from Your love. I am fully forgiven. I give You my life and give up trying to live on my own. Heal my heart and my life. I believe I am no longer alone. My heart is no longer orphaned, for I am Your child. I am free to live a new life—my old life died with Christ on the cross—I am now free to live a resurrected life. Thank you, Father, in Jesus' name.

Your past does not have to define your future. Romans 8:5 says, *"Those who trust God's action in them find that God's Spirit is in them—living and breathing God!"* The Holy Spirit *"touches our spirit and confirms who we really are …[God's] children"* (Romans 8:16). With God's Spirit living inside of us, we are free to live like Adam and God originally did, living as dear friends and close confidants.

God created us to be close to Him, as an adoring father with his beloved child. David spoke of this when he said, *"You watched me grow from conception to birth; all the stages of my life were spread out before You"* (Psalm 139:16). He's crazy about you. He's always thinking about you! *"How precious are your thoughts about me, O God! They are innumerable! I can't even count them; they outnumber the grains of sand!"* (Psalm 139:15). God's that in love with you! He's so smitten, and He promises to *"never leave you"* (John 14:16 NLV).

God wants to guide you through life by His written Word and the Spirit's direct guidance (Psalm 143:10, John 14:16). So get ready for a life of indescribable freedom, adventure, and rich conversational friendship because this *"resurrection life you received from God is not a timid, grave-tending life. It's adventurously expectant, greeting God with a childlike 'What's next, Papa?'"* (Romans 8:15).

Those who embrace the *"amazing grace of the Master, Jesus Christ, the extravagant love of God, the intimate friendship of the Holy Spirit"* (II Corinthians 13:14) will experience an unsurpassable love affair of the heart.

After drinking in long drafts of the Divine's love, your heart will be totally satisfied. But I must warn you, because you may find yourself so spoiled by the richness of heaven's affection that earthly love becomes far too bland for your taste. Some of you may even find yourself somewhat disappointed when you hear the Divine Matchmaker say, *"It's not good for [you] to be alone"* (Genesis 2:18). I was disappointed ... well, maybe only a little.

Letting God look under the hood of your heart and fix a few things may be a little uncomfortable, revealing, and momentarily painful, but we can be sure that *"If we go through the hard times with Him, then we're certainly going to go through the good times with Him!"* (Romans 8:17).

In life we have two choices: we can pay now and play later or we can play now and pay later. Pay the price to let God have all the time He needs alone with you and your heart. Trust me, there will be a price to pay. Many of my family and friends did not understand why I was more infatuated with God than with finding a girlfriend. They swore I was going to be a priest! They thought my standards were too high and that I would never find a woman who could meet them. I was made fun of, even by my Christian friends. They said I was missing out on so much, and in fact, I was missing out on the countless heart break I saw them endure. Years later, some of them are still reeling from the wreck of a rash relationship.

Don't head out onto the road of romance prematurely, with a heart running on only half its cylinders. Let your heavenly Father overhaul your heart, soul, and emotions first. Better to pay the price now and enjoy love's great ride for a lifetime than to find yourself broken down somewhere along the way.

CHAPTER FIVE

THE BACHELORETTE
(FOR WOMEN ~~ONLY~~ and men!)

"Loneliness and the feeling of being unwanted is the most terrible poverty."

— Mother Teresa

"People with their minds set on you, you keep completely whole, steady on their feet, because they keep at it and don't quit."

— Isaiah 26:3

"Cause when you're fifteen and somebody tells you they love you,
You're gonna believe them."

— Taylor Swift, "Fifteen"

F or many ladies, being single is a dreadful thing. We hate spending any holiday alone. We loathe Valentine's Day, yet we can't resist the candy isle abundantly overflowing with little chocolate hearts, often buying them for ourselves! We dreadfully, begrudgingly, and painfully enter the words "single" in the relationship status portion of our Facebook profile. We spend much of our single season dreaming about Prince Charming and our wedding day. The color of our bridesmaid dresses and our children's gender, names, and hair color are picked out long before the groom! So many of us waste so much time on broken hearts and monotonous crushes and spend endless days wondering if that cute Christian guy we met last night is the one. Hours tick by as we wait by the phone, wondering if it's the night he will call.

What if I told you that your season of singleness didn't have to be this way? It can be full of fun and laughter, great friendships, nights of popcorn and movies, midnight runs with your girlfriends to the grocery store for cartons of Rocky Road ice cream to go with that juicy chick-flick that is sure to bring tears to your eyes.

> Hey guys, this is Joel. Have you ever felt completely in the dark when it comes to understanding how the female mind works? This chapter will give you greater insight into how women see the world and see you! The chapter was written for women, by a woman (Casey). And in the following pages you will not only learn more about how women think and what they want, but you will unearth some indispensable tools you'll need—if you're going to successfully navigate down the road of romance with a woman! So buckle up and put it into 4-wheel drive! You are about to enter a place few men have dared to go before—the female mind!

You see, I believe God has given us ladies a specific season of singleness to prepare us for marriage, yet we waste so many of those years wondering when Prince Charming will ride in on his white horse. I once heard the statement, "Two halves do not make a whole when it comes to relationships," and boy is that true. Many marriages have failed because the skeletons in the closet were never addressed and popped out when least expected.

While it is impossible to address all the issues in your life, it is still important that many of those issues be addressed prior to being united in marriage. Trust me, those skeletons in the closet will come back to haunt you if you don't deal with them now.

And this is why maximizing your season of singleness comes into play. For many years, I held the philosophy that I would rather spend the rest of my life single than married to the wrong person. I had seen too many couples miserable in their marriages: girls who settled for less because they were desperate to get married, domineering woman who married passive men, and marriages that eventually led to ugly divorces.

I was perfectly happy being single. I had a great group of girlfriends, I loved my job, I enjoyed traveling the country and watching thousands of teenagers surrender their lives to Christ, and I cherished my time traveling the world and working in such places as the Mother Teresa Homes in Calcutta, India. Besides, what man could compete with Jesus, right? Life has too much to offer to spend it with the wrong person. I had determined I would rather journey through life alone than go through it miserable.

So, needless to say, I had pretty high standards for my Prince Charming. My family used to say that I wore a white glove when inspecting the guys in my life. They were convinced I was going to be a nun, but I knew my prince was out there and when he came along, I wanted to make sure I was ready!

Like many ladies, I too had a list of preconditions that needed to be met in order to win my heart. But what a tragedy it would be if my Prince Charming, meeting all the prerequisites on my list, passed me up because I fell short of the requirements on his list. I knew if I wanted an amazing man of God who was noble, honorable, admirable, strong in leadership and character, well liked and respected, charming, and good looking (of course, it wouldn't hurt), then I was going to need to be a woman worthy of that man's heart.

Instead of squandering my season of singleness on worthless crushes, pointless daydreams, and endless nights questioning if he's the one, I decided I was going to spend my time chasing after the woman God was calling me to be. If Proverbs 31 was the standard, I wanted to exceed it. Wholeness was the goal, and while being ready for my prince was not my focus, God certainly helped push me in that direction. I spent four years single, pursing wholeness and enjoying every day of it. Along the way I believe I discovered six essential steps that every woman must master during her season of singleness.

So, buckle up ladies, because I believe God is getting you ready for the ride of your life.

1)—EMOTIONAL STABILITY

Proverbs 31:25 says, *"Strength and dignity are her clothing and her position is strong and secure."* The lady in this verse defined what it means to be emotionally stable. I have often heard comparisons made between a guy's struggle with lust and a woman's struggle with her emotions.

Let's face it ladies, we are emotional beings, and while God created us to be that way, we often allow our emotions to get the best of us. I believe the first step toward wholeness and the key to guarding your heart is finding emotional stability.

To better understand the concept of emotional stability, let's look to the *Webster's Dictionary*. It defines the word "emotional" as an adjective relating to a person's emotions:

  ◌ Arousing or characterized by intense feeling
  ◌ Having feelings that are easily exited and openly displayed
  ◌ Based on emotion rather than reason

Webster's defines "stable" as:

  ◌ Not likely to change or fail: Firmly established
  ◌ Steady and not liable to change or move
  ◌ Sane and sensible; not easily upset or disturbed
  ◌ Not likely to give way or overturn; firmly fixed
  ◌ Having a calm and steady temperament, rather than being excitable or given to apparently irrational behavior.

As single women, the idea of a relationship is constantly knocking on the door of our minds. When you are emotionally stable, it is much easier to remain steady in the midst of all the emotions a relationship may bring. You can keep a sound mind while evaluating if he is right for you.

Many girls get lost in the idea of a relationship. They experience a flood of emotions at the first glimpse of attention from the opposite gender, and that flood of emotions causes them to make decisions they later regret. I am not saying it is wrong to have feelings for a guy or be attracted to him, it is what you do with those feelings that really matters. When you lack emotional stability, you often base your decisions on feelings rather than on reason.

I have met a lot of strong Christian girls who, in the heat of the moment, made a bad decision because they listened to emotion rather than reason or logic. We are constantly bombarded with the thoughts of, "If it feels good, do it!" leading us to believe our actions are void of consequences. As ladies, we must learn to embrace the blessings of emotions while standing firm on the bedrock of truth.

Now, I am not saying that we become like robots, void of all emotion. Feelings are a good thing. The Bible says Jesus was moved with compassion (Matthew 9:35). While emotions are a good thing, created by God, our emotions often change, but the truth never changes.

Becoming emotionally stable is learning to reason with a sound mind and to listen to wisdom over emotions. When emotion tells you to get lost in his eyes, reason tells you to evaluate his character. While emotion tells you hanging out alone in a room together isn't going to hurt anything, a sound mind tells you not to put yourself in a compromising situation. When emotion tells you a kiss isn't going to go any further, wisdom tells you one kiss is all it takes.

Emotional stability does not only apply to relationships, it applies to all areas of our lives. It is the foundation for many things we ladies struggle with, such as self-esteem, peer pressure, and other insecurities that are constantly coming at us. It is learning how to listen to wisdom and the Word of God instead of the emotional thoughts that bombard our mind.

Too often, girls wrap how they see themselves entirely in what other people, particularly guys, think of them. We allow pop culture to dictate what is physically acceptable and even go as far as starving ourselves to conform to the "norm." If we are rejected by a guy, we feel as if we are fat and ugly. If we are liked by a guy, we feel as if we are on top of the world. If we are accepted by a certain group of friends at school, we feel that must mean we are somehow good enough!

This flood of emotion can be irrational and based solely on feelings rather than on truth. We must learn to base our emotions on a bedrock of truth, the Word of God. While the world tells me I am too fat, too skinny, too short, or too tall, the Bible tells me I am fearfully and wonderfully made, knit together in my mother's womb (Psalm 139:13). God knows every hair on my head, and I am the apple of His eye (Psalm 17:8).

So, when you are rejected by that cute guy you liked so much, instead of starving yourself for three days, go back to the truth, the Word of God! You are fearfully and wonderfully made (Psalm 139:14).

Emotional stability is a constant steadiness, firmness, solidity, and a permanence of strength when it comes to your emotions. Amidst the rough and choppy emotional waters, you are able to remain anchored and stable.

I want to encourage you to use your season of singleness to become an emotionally stable woman, a woman with a sound mind and heart. Believe me, you will experience a flood of emotions when that special someone comes along and you want to make sure you are firmly established.

I believe emotional stability is the foundation for the other principles. If you are firmly established when it comes to your emotions, you can weather any storm. So, how do you become emotionally stable? There are three simple steps that helped me.

#1 Take every thought captive!

"The world is unprincipled. It's dog-eat-dog out there! The world doesn't fight fair. But we don't live or fight our battles that way—never have and never will. The tools of our trade aren't for marketing or manipulation, but they are for demolishing that entire massively corrupt culture. We use our powerful God—tools for smashing warped philosophies, tearing down barriers erected against the truth of God, fitting every loose thought and emotion and impulse into the structure of life shaped by Christ. Our tools are ready at hand for clearing the ground of every obstruction and building lives of obedience into maturity" (2 Corinthians 10:5).

I love how the Bible references using God's powerful tools for smashing warped philosophies. So, when culture tries to tell us ladies that beauty is on the cover of *Vogue* magazine, sex is cool and everyone is doing it, and you MUST have a boyfriend, we simply take captive those thoughts, smash those warped philosophies, and choose to believe God's Word.

When our mind is running rampant concerning a particular guy, "Does he like me? Am I pretty enough for him?" we again need to imprison those thoughts and line them up with God's Word.

#2 Get God's Word in your heart!

Psalm 119:9-16 says: *"How can a young person live a clean life? By carefully reading the map of your Word. I'm single-minded in pursuit of you; don't let me miss the road signs you've posted. I've banked your promises in the vault of my heart so I won't sin myself bankrupt. Be blessed, God; train me in your ways of wise living. I'll transfer to my lips all the counsel that comes from your mouth; I delight far more in what you tell me about living than in gathering a pile of riches. I ponder every morsel of wisdom from you, I attentively watch how you've done it. I relish everything you've told me of life, I won't forget a word of it."*

Whenever we have thoughts bombarding us—I'm too fat, too skinny, too ugly, not cool or popular enough—we need to remind ourselves of what God's Word says about us. When we are tempted by the opposite gender, we have to remind ourselves what God's Word says about purity.

Something I would encourage you to do is memorize at least five scriptures in each area you struggle with. For example, if you struggle with your self-image, memorize scriptures about how God sees you. If you struggle with temptations concerning the opposite gender, memorize scriptures about purity.

I have listed some scriptures at the end of this chapter that were really helpful for me. By hiding God's Word in your heart, you will learn to walk by truth and not by your feelings.

#3 Choose to be accountable!

Proverbs 27:17 (NIV) says, *"As iron sharpens iron, so one man sharpens another."*

We were not created to live in this world alone, in isolation. We need each other. There was only one person who walked this earth in complete and utter perfection, and that was Jesus. We, on the other hand, are not perfect, and need help to steer clear of sin. There is no shame in admitting your struggles to a close friend who can pray for you and encourage you when you are down. This is the essence of accountability.

When I made the commitment not to date until I met a man worthy of my heart, I had a circle of girlfriends with similar standards who held me accountable. Those same girls were bridesmaids at my wedding, watched me experience the first time I kissed Joel on our wedding day, and are still some of my best friends today. It is important that you find a circle of girls with similar values, standards, and goals who can hold you accountable.

Here are a few guidelines that will help you in your search for accountability partners:

- Your accountability partner(s) needs to be the same gender and approximately the same age.

- While it is important to have a group of girls your age, I would also suggest having a group of older women, mentors, you can talk to as well. Oftentimes, they have been through your very same circumstances and can provide wisdom for navigating through your situation.

- Make sure they are trustworthy and you feel comfortable sharing anything and everything with them.

- Have a commitment of trust between each other. Make an agreement that what is shared among you will not leave that circle. It is important to feel an absolute sense of trust with each other.

- Have a commitment to honesty. What good is accountability if you are not completely honest with each other? Remember, they are there to help you, not hurt you, so it is important that you share honestly with them.

- Ask follow-up questions. Call them in the middle of the week to see how they are doing in that particular area and bring it up the next time you see them.

- End each meeting with prayer and encouragement. I was also committed to praying for each one of my accountability partners on a daily basis.

- Meet on a weekly basis. Perhaps after youth group or after school one day you could go out for a smoothie or coffee, or you could meet at one of your friend's houses. Even if you are only able to talk on the phone for that week, make sure you are checking in with each other on a weekly basis.

For some of you, these standards may sound extreme, but I want to encourage you—when you make a commitment to remain pure until marriage, the enemy will throw every kind of attack your way. 1 Peter 5:8 says, *"Be well balanced (temperate, sober of mind), be vigilant and cautious at all times; for that enemy of yours, the devil, roams around like a lion roaring [in fierce hunger], seeking someone to seize upon and devour"* (Amplified).

It is a battlefield when you choose to follow Christ, so you must take every precaution necessary if you are serious about remaining pure.

Now that you have the tools to master emotional stability, let's move onto the second essential step, sexual purity.

2)—Sexual Purity

Ladies, for many years I bought into the world's lie that *MTV, Melrose Place,* and *90210* really knew what they were talking about when it came to sex. I thought to be accepted, to have an awesome dating relationship and sex life, I had to follow the examples on TV. I thought the world had it all right when it came to sex, but I was completely wrong.

You see, the One who really knows what He is talking about when it comes to sex, the One who knows how to have a great sex life, is God. He's the one who created it!

What a crazy concept, right? When you think about the way the world has perverted sex, it is difficult to imagine that God invented it. God gave us this amazing gift called sex, this hot, passionate, exciting, and incredible gift. (I can say that, I'm married! It's awesome!)

In Genesis 1, God commands us to be fruitful and multiply, and in the next chapter it says man and woman became one flesh. God gave us sex to share the deepest, most intimate part of us with the person we will spend forever with. It is the deepest expression of who we are, created to bond you with your husband. What a beautiful gift!

The trouble with sex comes when we take this amazing gift that God meant for marriage and use it outside of marriage.

I like to think of sex a lot like a fire inside of a fireplace. Nothing beats snuggling up to a hot fire on a cold, rainy day! It's warm, cozy, and when the fire is inside of the fireplace, you don't fear its danger.

Now, when you take that warm, cozy, hot fire outside of that fireplace and put it in the middle of your living room floor, you better run for your life! You now have a dangerous situation on your hands. That once cozy fire is now threatening your house and your life!

Sex is a lot like that. Inside of marriage, it is warm, cozy, it feels great, and it's safe. But outside of marriage, it's dangerous. When you take sex outside of marriage, you face some serious consequences. The world has painted the picture that sex before marriage is void of consequences and they often show you the fun and exciting side of sex, but let's face it, the girl left with a broken heart, pregnant, or with an STD just doesn't sell well, now does it? Sex sells, but not the consequences of it. So, girls, let's dive a little deeper into the consequences of sex before marriage.

Let's start with the big STD! Now, most of you reading this know what a sexually transmitted disease is, but just in case it slipped your mind, I thought I would refresh your memory. Sexually transmitted diseases are infections caused by bacteria, viruses, and parasites (as in, little bugs … down there!), which can produce acute symptoms like irritating vaginal discharge, painful pelvic inflammatory disease, and potentially fatal ectopic pregnancy.

OK, that's just gross! Ladies, next time you have this really cute guy with those bulging muscles and big dreamy eyes telling you, "Baby, I love you. I want to spend forever with you. Let's have sex!" This is what I want each and every one of you to say to him: "I don't know what kind of junk you've got growing in your trunks, and I don't know where you have been or who you have been with, so no thanks!"

I don't know about you, but the idea of little bugs, down south, is enough to keep my zipper, up north!

Oftentimes, people think they will never contract an STD, but I am sure the 19 million people currently living with a STD did not intentionally sign up for it. I am sure that the 65 million people currently living with an incurable STD (meaning, there isn't a cure!) didn't deliberately contract them. I can assure you that most of those people thought it would never happen to them. (Go to www.womenshealth.gov and U.S. Department of Health & Human services, www.urologychannel.com.)

I must also warn you that STDs most commonly occur in sexually active teenagers and young adults. Statistics reveal that 1 in 2 sexually-active young people will contract a STD by the age of 25, and 1 in 4 teenage girls are currently infected with a STD! We must not be naïve in believing it will never happen to us. All it takes is just one time. (Go to www.SADD.org and Federal Center for disease control www.msnbc. msn.com/id/ 23574940.)

Another consequence of having sex before marriage is pregnancy. Approximately 1 million teenagers become pregnant every year, and that means 2,800 teenage girls get pregnant every single day! Approximately 4 in 10 young women in the U.S. will become pregnant at least once before the age of 20. (Go to www.menstuff.org/issues/byissue/teenpregnancy .html#onemillionandwww.troubledteens.com/troubled-teens-statistics. html.)

Now, don't get me wrong, I think pregnancy is the greatest thing in the whole entire world! When my husband and I had our first child, I will never forget the moment we discovered we were pregnant. I purchased a home pregnancy test at Wal-mart and when I got home, I stood in anticipation as I waited for the results, just hoping that two pink lines would appear. The first one appeared immediately and seconds later a pale pink line emerged. I was pregnant! Utter bliss does not describe the emotion we felt in that moment. We hugged, kissed, and jumped for joy at the thought of the new addition to our family.

Ladies, not once did I wonder if Joel was going to stick around to raise this child. Not once did I worry if he was going to provide for us. Not once did I wonder, "Who's my baby's daddy?"

Yet, in the midst of all the excitement, I could not help but think of the thousands of teenage girls who watch those two pink lines appear and feel devastation and fear instead of excitement and joy. Instead of rejoicing, they are thinking, "Is my boyfriend going to break up with me when he finds out? How will we provide for this child? Who is my baby's daddy?" Girls who feel so devastated many times believe abortion is their only way out.

Let me pause for just a moment, ladies, if you are facing pregnancy now, I want each of you to know that no matter how severe your circumstances, the God we serve is a great and mighty God who can get you through any challenge. Though being pregnant out of wedlock is not an ideal situation, God will get you through it. He desires to take what the enemy meant for evil and turn it to good. Please do not ever feel that abortion is your only way out. That child is a wonderful blessing from God. He loves and cares for your child, and do not let anyone tell you that life does not begin at conception.

I will never forget feeling Lincoln move inside of me or seeing him on the sonogram machine for the first time. I could see his fingers, his toes, his spine, and I could even see him sucking his thumb. Tears welled up in my eyes as I thought of the millions of babies with toes, fingers, and spines, who enjoyed sucking their thumbs and loved the comfort of their mommy's tummy who are aborted every year.

If you are facing pregnancy out of wedlock and do not know what to do, I want to encourage you to speak with a pastor or someone you trust at your church. Remember, you are not in this alone and you do not have to face these circumstances alone.

And if you have had an abortion and are still living with the regret of your decision, I want you to know God is a gracious and forgiving God. He is ready and waiting, with open arms, to heal and forgive you.

Now, while I enjoyed pregnancy and have loved every single day of motherhood, I would never wish that upon an unmarried teenager. I am not exaggerating when I tell you that it was one of the hardest things I have ever gone through. Teenage mothers are less likely to finish high school or college, and it is estimated that as much as 80% of unwed teen mothers end up on welfare. That's no Jamie Lynn Spears fantasy, ladies, that's a reality! Teenage pregnancy is a serious consequence you can face when you have sex before marriage. (Go to www.dosomething.org/tipsand-tucks/ background-teenage-gregnancy.)

Many of you might be thinking to yourself, "That won't happen to me because I use protection." First of all, condoms are not 100% guaranteed to protect you, and secondly, they don't make a condom to protect your heart.

The Bible explains in Genesis 2:24 that when we have sex with someone, the two of you become one. What that means is that sex comes with strings attached. When we give our bodies, our hearts will follow. I once heard the analogy of arriving at the altar on your wedding day, but all you have to give the man God created for you is a beat up, busted heart that has been trampled on by your previous relationships. I don't know about you, but I wanted to save my heart for the man God had for me.

Listen to this:

"There's more to sex than mere skin on skin. Sex is as much a spiritual mystery as physical fact. As written in Scripture, "The two become one." Since we want to become spiritually one with the Master, we must not pursue the kind of sex that avoids commitment and intimacy, leaving us more lonely than ever-the kind of sex that can never "become one." There is a sense in which sexual sins are different from all others. In

sexual sin we violate the sacredness of our own bodies, these bodies that were made for God-given and God-modeled love, for "becoming one" with another. Or didn't you realize that your body is a sacred place, the place of the Holy Spirit? Don't you see that you can't live however you please; squandering what God paid such a high price for? The physical part of you is not some piece of property belonging to the spiritual part of you. God owns the whole works. So let people see God in and through your body." (1 Corinthians 6:16-20)

I realize that remaining pure in the midst of a culture that is constantly bombarding you with sex is an uphill battle. It seems that everywhere you turn, from TV to music and from ads to magazines, sex is constantly in your face. You can't even walk through the mall without being reminded that Victoria has no more secrets!

When I gave my life over to Christ, technically I was still a virgin, but I sure didn't feel like one. I had made many mistakes in my past that left me feeling stained and worthless. I felt as if I was not worthy of a godly man because of my past mistakes, but God quickly reminded me of how forgiving He is.

You see, the beautiful thing about God is that He not only forgives, He also forgets. The Bible says that He casts our sins as far as the east is from the west, and though we were stained as red as crimson, He has washed us as white as snow. My heavenly Father has forgiven and washed me clean, which meant that I was worth waiting for. After all, I am a daughter of the King!

Maybe some of you have felt the same way because of your past mistakes. Whether you have given your purity away or done other sexual things that have left you feeling disqualified from God's best, I want you to know that those feelings of shame are lies from the pit of hell. God is ready and willing, waiting with open arms, to forgive you, set you free, and wash you clean from your past. He is just waiting for you to ask. So, if you are sitting there reading this chapter and feeling stained, but ready for God's forgiveness, I want you to find a private spot right now, just you and God, and pray this with me:

Heavenly Father, I am so sorry for my past mistakes, please forgive me. (Be specific in your request for forgiveness.) Forgive me for giving my purity away, wash me clean, and restore me. I know now that I was searching for love in a place it could not be found, but I turn to You to be filled with Your love. I know that You accept and receive me now with arms open wide. You no longer see my past mistakes, but instead see a pure and spotless daughter. Help me to believe this and walk in this truth every day. In Jesus' name, Amen.

Now that you are forgiven and washed clean, it is time for a fresh start. I must warn you that God never said it would be easy; He just said it would be worth it! When I made the decision to stay pure until marriage, I knew it would be difficult, but it was truly worth it.

So, we end this section with a decision: Will you choose to remain pure until marriage? If so, would you take some time and make that commitment to God. Pray this with me:

Heavenly Father, I choose from this day forward to remain pure until marriage. I know that I am your child and worth waiting for. I know you have an amazing relationship and marriage for me someday, and from this day forward I will walk in your purity. God, would you give me the strength, in the midst of many temptations and pressures, to remain pure. Surround me with sisters to hold me accountable and brothers to guard my heart. In Jesus' name I pray, Amen!

I want to give you a few tips that might help you on your journey of purity:

#1 Don't put yourself in compromising situations.

Let me give you an example: When Joel and I were courting, we were never in a house alone together or in a room alone together with the door closed. We did not ride in a car alone together after dark and spent much of our time in public places, like Barnes and Noble or Starbucks.

#2 Remain accountable.

It is always easier to remain strong when you hang out with like-minded people.

#3 Take a break from dating.

If you have struggled sexually in the past, I want to encourage you to take a break from dating relationships. For how long? My suggestion would be a full year. This will allow you plenty of time to get strong in that area.

#4 Memorize purity scriptures.

Last, but certainly not least, memorize purity scriptures. I have also included a purity commitment form at the end of this chapter. I encourage you to fill it out and hang it up in your room or somewhere you can see it, to remind yourself that you are worth the wait!

3)—DeVeLoPiNG HeaLTHY FRieNDSHiPS

The third essential step you must master during your season of singleness is developing healthy friendships with the opposite gender. I really learned the true meaning of this when I was an intern at Teen Mania. The first year we were not allowed to date, which permitted healthy friendships to flourish between guys and girls.

It may sound difficult at first, but what I found was that it took away the pressure of "does he like me ... do I like him?" This was really nice for a change. We have all had those awkward friendships where the guy has a crush on you but you don't like him, or vice versa. There's nothing more embarrassing than being relegated to the let's-just-be-friends category. Often, you meet girls who, because of previous hurts or betrayals, only know how to develop friendships with guys. And then there are the girls whose relationship radar never seems to turn off—there is a constant beeping every time a remotely cute guy walks into view, and seconds later they are on to the next bachelor.

While these behaviors often come as second nature to ladies, we must overcome the odds and learn to develop healthy friendships with the fellas.

Prior to my commitment not to date, my male friendships always ended in heartbreak of some sort. I didn't understand how to guard their heart, or my heart for that matter. They would either have a crush on me, but I didn't like them in that way, or vice versa, which often resulted in a ruined friendship. After becoming an intern at Teen Mania, I learned how to have great male friends without developing feelings for them, and though I was not perfect, I learned to guard their hearts as well as mine.

There were a few guidelines that I followed to assure my heart and their hearts would be guarded:

#1 Watch what you say.

For starters, I was careful of the information I shared. Ladies are blessed with the incredible gift of emotion, which often means when we share our hearts with people, we develop some sort of fondness for that person. Often, we spend hours on the phone with our guy friends sharing the deepest parts of who we are and then wonder why feelings have developed.

I would try to only share with my male friends what I would feel comfortable sharing in a group. So, if I didn't feel comfortable sharing it with a large group of people I somewhat knew, I would not share it one-on-one with my male friends.

#2 Guard your time.

I tried to limit the amount of time I spent alone with my guy friends and always remained in public places with them. Now, I am not saying it is wrong to spend time alone with a guy, but you must keep in mind that time equals relationship. Some of my most precious memories were times I spent with my guy friends in large groups. I also chose not to ride in a car alone with a guy unless it was an absolute necessity.

I am not saying this is a must for everyone or that I was perfect, but I always tried to guard my heart and their hearts. I once had a friend who shared an analogy that stuck with me. She explained that your guy friends are someone's future husband, so you need to guard their hearts like you would want your sisters in Christ to guard your future husband's heart. What that means is to treat your male friends like you would want your future husband to be treated.

I have often been asked, "If you never spend time alone with a guy, how do you know if he is the one?" and "If you don't date, how will you ever find someone?"

Joel and I will dive into this a little more in the following chapters, but that is why friendship is so important. I knew exactly what I wanted in a husband and was not willing to compromise. When you develop a friendship with a guy in healthy group settings, you are able to evaluate his character, interest, likes, and dislikes, which will allow you to see if he is a potential for you. At that point, there are healthy ways to proceed, which we will also address in the chapters to come.

#3 Develop healthy friendships with other girls.

It is also important to learn how to develop healthy friendships with the same gender. I am a girl and understand that my fellow sisters often struggle with gossip and cattiness, but we must learn to find and develop friendships with amazing, godly women.

A mentor once shared with me how relationships with the opposite gender change dramatically after marriage. It is no longer appropriate to have long, heartfelt phone conversations or lunch dates with your guy friends. You now hang out in groups or with couples. Imagine how you would feel if your husband had a great girl friend he shared all his cares with! I don't know about you, but I want to be that great girl friend he shares his heart with.

I am not saying it is wrong to have guy friends after marriage, and you certainly will, but the dynamic of those friendships definitely change after you get married.

4)—Determine Your Physical Standards

The fourth essential step you must take during your season of singleness is to determine your physical standards. We often make mistakes because we have not established our boundaries. Many relationships have failed because of physical decisions made in the heat of the moment.

Developing your physical standards while you are in a relationship is good, but it is much wiser to determine your standards before a relationship ever begins. We normally feel a flood of emotions at the beginning of a relationship and tend to make decisions based on emotion instead of reason. If you have your physical standards determined before entering into that relationship, you will not be as tempted to give way.

For example, I did not want to kiss until my wedding day. Things normally progress pretty fast after kissing and I knew I didn't want to go down that road. I had that standard long before I met Joel, and amazingly, Joel felt the same way. Although you may not agree completely with the other person's standards, it is still important to respect their standards.

Because Joel and I chose not to kiss until our wedding day, every physical step felt like a big deal. So, when we first started courting, I was extremely excited to hold hands. After Joel had asked me to court him, he immediately set our physical boundaries and included in those was not holding hands. He felt it would be best to wait until engagement to take that step.

While I was slightly disappointed, purity was the aim and respecting his physical standards was way more important to me. Remember that every person and relationship is different. You may think that mine and Joel's physical standards were too extreme, and that is perfectly fine, but it is important to determine what your boundaries and standards are (and they should line up with God's Word).

Before meeting Joel, I had a list of non-negotiable standards, things that I felt were from the Lord that I was not willing to budge on. Then I had a list of preferences of which were open for discussion, like holding hands. I have listed a few things below and I encourage you to pray and determine your standards on each one of these and at what point in the relationship you would feel comfortable with them. Remember, it is not a list of "rules" but rather guidelines that will help you honor God through your purity.

- **Hugging / Embracing / Snuggling**

- **Lying down together**

- **Holding Hands**

- **Kissing** (If you feel comfortable with kissing, determine how much, when, and for how long. For example, is it a peck on the lips, forehead, or cheek? Will you kiss whenever or only before you say goodbye. How long will you allow the kiss to last?)

  - **Being alone** (Is it OK to be together in a house, room, or car?)

  - **Curfew** (How late is too late to stay out together? As we get tired, our judgment is often times blurred.)

I realize that some people may find this a bit radical, but remaining pure until marriage is difficult. Taking the time to determine your standards, based on the Word of God, prior to getting into a relationship will help set you up for success.

5)—WHAT'S YOUR VISION?

The fifth step you must master during your season of singleness is to find a vision for your life. You have to know where you are going in life before you determine who you are going to be with along life's journey.

If God is calling you to be a full-time missionary to Africa, but the guy you're with wants to be a pastor in the U.S., you might run into a few problems along the way. Take some time to seek God for the vision He has for your life.

I have listed a few questions below that will help you discover what God is calling you to do. I encourage you to pray and search deep in your heart for the answers to these questions:

- What is your greatest passion in life?

- What are your talents?

- Would you like to be in full-time ministry or would you like a career in business, medicine, politics, etc?

- If you would like to be in full-time ministry, what type of ministry would you like to be involved in? Do you want to work in the US, overseas, or both?

- If in full-time ministry, what type of people would you like to work with: children, singles, youth, young adults?

- If you are planning to pursue a career outside of ministry, how would you use that for God's glory and to help His people?

- Are you interested in going to college? If so, what are you interested in majoring in and what are your top five colleges?

These are just a few questions that will help you discover what God is calling you to do. There is no better time than when you are single to discover all that God has for you.

I once worked with a woman who married later in life. She had her master's degree, worked full time for a ministry, traveled the world, and even met Mother Teresa! She is now married with three beautiful children and has since told me that she felt as if she was able to live two full lives.

When she was single, she traveled the world and pursued every dream on her heart, and now that she is married she is a wife and mother and absolutely loves it! She maximized her season of singleness, and I pray you will, too.

6)—Make Your Dream List

Last, but certainly not least, is to make a dream list. How will you know if he is right for you if you don't know what it is you are looking for? This is a serious question, because we are talking about the rest of your life! Settling is not an option!

Quite often, when I suggest making a dream list, people automatically think I am talking about physical attributes. While I am not saying you should disregard the outer appearance, what is on the inside is much more important.

When I made a dream list, I wanted a man of honor, integrity, and noble character. I wanted someone who loved God more than anything else. I wanted him to be a man of his word, always doing the right thing. I wanted someone trustworthy, a good listener, easy to talk to, and someone who was fun and made me laugh. I wanted a man who respected and honored me, who treated me like I was a daughter of God (the way a lady should be treated). I wanted someone with a college degree, a stable job, and a vision for his life. I knew I needed a man who was a strong leader and not intimidated by a strong woman. I told the Lord that tall, dark, and handsome wouldn't hurt either, and man, did He deliver!

I have listed a few questions that will help you evaluate and discover what type of guy (or girl, for you fellas) you desire:

- **Faith** (Is he a born again, on-fire-for-God Christian who loves God more than anyone you have ever met? This is the most important question you will ever ask yourself when it comes to evaluating if a guy is right for you. The Bible is very specific about not being unequally yoked (2 Corinthians 6:14). By dating someone who is not a Christian, you are inviting all sorts of problems into your relationship.)

- **Religion** (While you both may be Christians, it is also important to share the same major doctrinal beliefs.)

- **Vision** (Can you submit, help, and follow the vision God has placed on his life and does it line up with the vision for your life?)

- **Character** (This is a must as well. Evaluating his character is extremely important. Is he loyal and kind? How does he treat others around him? How does he treat you? Is he honest? These are all important questions to ask.)

- **Education** (Is a college degree important to you?)

- **Family** (Does he want a family someday? Do you?)

These are just a few questions to get you started. It is important to search your heart and discover your desires for a spouse. It is perfectly fine to be specific with the Lord concerning the desires of your heart.

I remember telling the Lord that I really wanted someone who came from a broken family. I felt that was such a huge part of my life and to fully understand me, he needed to understand where I came from.

I would also encourage you to search the heart of God. He knows exactly what you need and desire before you even speak it. After all, He is the Divine Matchmaker.

My hope is that these words will help you better maximize your season of singleness. Instead of wasting precious time wondering if he is the one or when he will come, you can use this time to become all that God is calling you to be.

You will be so glad you did!

SCRIPTURES TO PUT TO MEMORY

Psalm 139:14 *"Oh Yes, you shaped me first inside, then out; you formed me in my mother's womb. I thank you, High God- you're breathtaking! Body and soul, I am marvelously made! I worship in adoration- what a creation! You know me inside and out, you know every bone in my body; you know exactly how I was made, bit by bit, how I was sculpted from nothing into something. Like an open book, you watched me grow from conception to birth; all the stages of my life were spread out before you, the days of my life all prepared before I'd even lived one day."*

Psalm 119:73 (Amplified) *"Your hands have made me, cunningly fashioned and established me; give me understanding, that I may learn Your commands."*

1 Samuel 16:7 *"But God told Samuel, "Looks aren't everything. Don't be impressed with his looks and stature. I've already eliminated him. God judges persons differently than humans do. Men and women look at the face, God looks into the heart."*

1 Peter 3:3-4 (NLV) *"Don't be concerned about the outward beauty of fancy hair styles, expensive jewelry, or beautiful clothes. You should clothe yourselves instead with the beauty that comes from within, the unfading beauty of a gentle and quiet spirit, which is so precious to God."*

Proverbs 31:30 (NLT) *"Charm is deceptive, and beauty does not last; but a woman who fears the Lord will be greatly praised."*

Psalm 17:8 (NIV) *"Keep me as the apple of your eye; hide me in the shadow of your wings."*

PURITY COMMITMENT FORM

I (write your name) _____ commit to emotional, physical, and sexual purity from this day forward (write today's date) _____. I choose to save my heart and body for the person God has for me until marriage.

I have forgiven myself for any past mistakes that I have made and realize God has also forgiven me. I receive the Lord's forgiveness and from this day forward, I commit to purity. I will save myself for marriage.

_____
(Your signature)

_____
(Your accountability partner's signature)

INTERMISSION:

SOME RULES FOR THE ROAD

"Guard your heart for it affects everything you do."
— Proverbs 4:23

"We're in no hurry, God. We're content to linger in the path sign-posted with your decisions. Who you are and what you've done are all we'll ever want."
— Isaiah 26:8

"I want you also to be smart, making sure every 'good' thing is the real thing."
— Romans 16:19

A fter the servant received the definitive heavenly sign—Rebekah watering his 10 camels—Scripture says that the servant silently watched and wondered if this was the one God planned for him to meet. The spotlight of heaven couldn't have shined more brightly on her, singling Rebekah out as the one for Isaac, yet the servant restrained himself from revealing this to her. Instead, he remained silent; he watched and he wondered, *"Was this God's answer?"* (Genesis 24:21). It is critical that we do the same when our prospective "pick" comes into focus.

I can't tell you how many times I have seen people rush into a committed relationship at the first fluttering of romantic feelings. They jump head first into the pool of passion, leaving wisdom poolside. When the initial flash of feelings fade and they see who it is they have chosen, many couples wish they had acted like Abraham's servant—taking the time to watch the other person's character, wait silently before the Lord, and ask if this is the one God intended them to meet.

As we mentioned earlier, the Bible warns, *"Above all else, guard your heart, for it affects everything you do"* (Proverbs 4:23 NLV). Who you choose to give your heart to is one of the most important decisions you will ever make. It will affect everything you do.

So, how exactly do you guard your heart like this proverb says? We'll talk specifics in the chapters to come, but a huge component of accomplishing this is simply holding tight to the way of wisdom. Traversing the road of romance can be a treacherous endeavor for your heart. On this road, your heart may experience the ride of a lifetime or, regrettably, completely crash and burn. Either way, the stakes are high.

If you attempt to travel this road, you must travel as wisely as possible. One of the best ways to do this is to gather as many principles as possible from the Word and from those who have successfully lived them out. Then, proceed with caution.

"Dear friend, take my advice; it will add years to your life. I'm writing out clear directions to Wisdom Way, I'm drawing a map to Righteous

Road. I don't want you ending up in blind alleys, or wasting time making wrong turns. Hold tight to good advice; don't relax your grip. Guard it well—your life is at stake! Don't take Wicked Bypass; don't so much as set foot on that road. Stay clear of it; give it a wide berth. Make a detour and be on your way ... The ways of right-living people glow with light; the longer they live, the brighter they shine. But the road of wrongdoing gets darker and darker—travelers can't see a thing; they fall flat on their faces. Learn it by Heart" (Proverbs 4:10-15, 18-19).

Wisdom will help you relish the intoxicating feelings that come with love, but keep you from becoming inebriated by them. If we are going to avoid painful detours and experience the road of right-living that causes a couple to shine brighter and brighter, then we must learn God's timeless principles *"by Heart."* This will require concentration, contemplation, and the utmost vigilance.

"Dear friend, listen well to my words; tune your ears to my voice. Keep my message in plain view at all times. Concentrate! Learn it by heart! Those who discover these words live, really live; body and soul, they're bursting with health. Keep vigilant watch over your heart; that's where life starts. Don't talk out of both sides of your mouth; avoid careless banter, white lies, and gossip. Keep your eyes straight ahead; ignore all sideshow distractions. Watch your step, and the road will stretch out smooth before you. Look neither right nor left; leave evil in the dust" (Proverbs 4:20-27).

In the next few chapters, Casey and I will share with you the route we took into our romantic relationship. We gathered as much advice and wisdom as we could before we set out on our road of romance and then we took our time savoring each stage of the process. We tried to follow Lady Wisdom's advice, *"First pay attention to me, and then relax. Now you can take it easy-you're in good hands"* (Proverbs 1:33).

Following her ways were so lovely, we didn't want to rush anything. Like having a multiple-course meal at an elegant restaurant, we wanted to take our time relishing each dish. We had seen too many people skip the entire meal and go straight for dessert. To us, not only did it seem unwise, but seemed to miss the whole point of sharing something spectacular together. Dessert is good, but so is the salad and the steak and all the other entrees. I figured if I didn't have to make a choice between just having dessert or the other courses, why skip ahead? I wanted to savor them all.

Our admonition is to take your time in every season, from single-hood, and God willing, on throughout your marriage. Appreciate each stage as it comes. After all, romance is not a destination; it's a journey. Enjoy it!

Romance is about sharing a lifetime with someone you can entrust your whole heart to—someone who loves you for just being you. It takes wisdom and time to discover if someone really loves you that authentically, and vice versa.

Even if you think you have a clear sign from heaven, it would still be wise to do as Abraham's servant did and take some time to silently watch and wonder if this is the one the Lord intended you to meet.

CHAPTER SIX

FRIENDING:

FRIENDSHIP IS THE FOUNDATION

"You've captured my heart, dear friend. You looked at me, and I fell in love. One look my way and I was hopelessly in love!"

— Song of Solomon 4:9

"We cannot really love anybody with whom we never laugh."

— Agnes Repplier

"You're more than a lover … you're my best friend."

— Tim McGraw, "My Best Friend"

I remember that night like it happened yesterday. It was the night I fell head-over-heels in love with Casey. A group of friends and I were hanging out at her apartment. Casey and I were sitting across the kitchen table discussing some of our favorite scriptures. As she opened her Bible and read a few verses that had recently peaked her interest. Something began to peak mine. I found myself not concentrating on the verses, but rather, on the way her beautiful brown eyes followed the lines of text she was reading.

"Wow," I thought. "Those are the most stunning eyes I've ever seen." She looked up at me momentarily. I hadn't heard one word she said, but I, nonetheless, nodded my head and said, "Hmm, that was really great." I was completely distracted by the way her long black eyelashes batted when she blinked. They were amazing, like twin ships sailing over glassy amber pools.

She continued, *"Even youth grow tired and weary, and young men stumble and fall; but those who hope ..."* I was thinking, "I really like how her lips pucker when she pronounces P-sounds." She was wearing some sort of chapstick or lip-gloss that made them slightly shimmer. Whatever it was, her lips were definitely looking easy-breezy-beautiful! *"... in the Lord will renew their strength."*

I thought, "Man, I could study the Bible with her all day!" And then, "Joel, grab a hold of yourself! She's reading Scripture for goodness sake ... wow, she really does have lovely brown hair." And then I said to myself, "Joel, you'd be an idiot not to marry this girl!"

I was seriously confused. Why were all these thoughts overriding my regularly rational thought process? We discussed the scriptures for a little while and then shortly after, I left. Something wild was happening in my heart. I had never felt this way about anyone before. As the old owl in Bambi concluded, "Everyone gets twitterpated." It was now happening to me.

I (Casey) will never forget the first night he came over to my house. I received a phone call from a friend who lived in my apartment complex. He asked if a friend of his could come over and borrow our computer. After we gladly accepted, he then dropped the bombshell that it was Joel Johnson!

Ladies, Joel was the most-eligible bachelor on Teen Mania's campus, not to mention he was extremely handsome, well respected, and was one of the most amazing men of God who has ever crossed my path! I must admit I was extremely nervous! While Joel met almost every qualification on my "wish list," I knew my heart was worth fighting for and I resisted the temptation to instantly give it over to him.

After he left that night, I went straight to my accountability partner. I was extremely attracted to Joel, both physically and spiritually, but I didn't want my emotions to get the best of me. That was the first of many hang-out times with Joel, and each time I made it a point to guard my thoughts and my heart!

I prayed about my friendship with Joel frequently and each time I felt the Lord directing me to just make myself available to his friendship, and to continue to guard my heart. I would always respond to Joel's requests, but I never pursued him. Often, girls take the leadership role in pursuing a guy they might be interested in, and then wonder why their hearts get broken. While Joel was an incredible man, I knew I was an incredible woman and any man who wanted to capture my heart must not only pursue it, but fight for it as well. Over time, my emotions became neutral and I thought of Joel as a great friend God had brought into my life, not as a potential romance.

I'm going to pause right here and backtrack a little before I explain what happened later on that evening. Up until that night, I was just somewhat interested in finding out who Casey was. Ron had given me a raving review of her character and told me that I needed to get to know her. We had a lot of mutual friends, so I maximized the opportunity by organizing some BBQs, group hang-out times, and prayer meetings, all in order to get to know Casey better.

I didn't want her to know I was even a little bit interested, because people show their best side when they like someone (or think someone they are interested in likes them). I wanted to see Casey around her friends, to see what she was about and who she really was. It's easy for anyone to act like someone they're not for an hour or two on a date, but it's harder to do that when you're around people who really know you. If you do act different than usual, your friends or family will give you a hard time. I didn't know much about Casey then, but I wanted to see the real her as best I could. I wanted to see her true colors and character. I thought hanging out with her in a large group of mutual friends would be the best way to accomplish this.

Now, let's get back to the story.

After I left Casey's apartment, I didn't head home. I went to a field where I often prayed. As I began to walk, I couldn't stop thinking about how much I enjoyed being around Casey. Our conversations were so full of life and we always had so much fun together. It was like our personalities just fit. I began to think that this is what it must feel like to fall in love.

I attempted to pray, trying to get some much-needed clarity concerning the feelings I was experiencing (and what I should do about them), but it was excruciatingly difficult to focus on anything ... except her. I loved the way she laughed and loved the Lord. I loved her strong personality. She lived by principles and genuine conviction. Yet, all her strength was embodied in the quintessence of graceful femininity. I had never met anyone like her. She was truly unique and I was hopelessly captivated.

I'd met all kinds of single women over the years, such as models, celebrities, spiritual leaders, rock stars, worship leaders, educators, party girls, and pastors daughters, yet none of them caused my heart to fall head-over-heals in love. Don't get me wrong, all these other women had beautiful and admirable attributes, but none of them had that mix of personality, physical beauty, emotional stability, and spiritual passion to unlock my heart the way Casey had. She was beautiful inside and out. She was in a class all her own. Proverbs 31:29 pretty much sums up what I was feeling: *"Many women have done wonderful things, but you've outclassed them all!"*

"I would be a fool not to marry this girl!" I whispered to myself. I started asking the Lord what I should do. I asked if I should pursue her. I heard no response, so I asked for wisdom concerning this relationship, knowing that *"if you need wisdom—if you want to know what God wants you to do—ask Him, and He will gladly tell you"* (James 1:5 NLV). Still, there was no reply, direction, or sign. I couldn't stop thinking about her.

I said it again, "God, I would be a fool not to marry this girl!" My heart was beating, my skin was tingling, and my mind was racing. I started quoting Proverbs 3:5-6, *"Trust in the Lord with all your heart, and lean not on your own understanding; In all your ways acknowledge Him, And He shall direct your paths*" (NKJV).

I was hoping that meditating on this would help me gain some control over my intellect. It did help some, but I still felt quite powerless in my efforts to resist the torrent of thoughts swirling in my brain. I exclaimed, "God, I would be an idiot not to marry this girl."

I was trying to be still and know that He is God, but I was failing miserably. I knew I desperately needed God's direction. I wasn't going to pursue Casey without guidance from the Divine Matchmaker. I had seen too many relationships wipe out and there was no way I was going to attempt to ride this wave of emotion without His expert advice. However, this did not change the fact that I had never met anyone like Casey and that I was extremely attracted to her.

I again repeated Proverbs 3:5-6, trying to calm the mental churning in my mind. I continued to pray for direction on what I should do, but I received no heavenly response. I continued to walk and pray for another 45 minutes. I must have quoted Proverbs 3:5-6 a 100 times, almost always followed by the statement, "God, I would be a fool not to marry this girl!"

Thoughts of Casey were whipping wildly around my mind, and solidifying my frustration was the fact that I seemed quite powerless to stop them. It seemed that getting God's perspective that night was unlikely. But then, like a blowtorch through butter, the voice of God cut through my near coagulated thoughts as He candidly said, "Joel, you won't be ready for a relationship until you are ready to get your will neutral to Mine."

Wow, that wasn't the response I had quite expected.

I left the field sober, yet encouraged. I had received some direction concerning the situation, even if it wasn't what I anticipated. Of course, God was totally right. My will was not neutral, and I knew that. I also knew that the first step to hearing God was a surrendered heart. If I could not get my will and heart neutral, then I would only be open to hearing an answer from God that would agree with what I wanted to hear.

It would be like someone going to his or her father to ask for his blessing to get married, but still planning on getting married anyway, no matter what the father said.

If your mind is already made up, there is no point in asking anyone for council. I recognized it would be pointless for me to ask my heavenly Father for guidance if my mind was already made up about Casey. I had to be surrendered to do whatever He wanted in order to get my will neutral. If not, I would just be going through the motions.

But complete surrender of your will is easier said than done. I prayed and fasted, but it still didn't break the emotional enchantment that Casey, unknowingly, held over my heart. About a month later, I headed overseas to New Zealand for three weeks of speaking engagements. From there, I flew home to California for a week to visit my family for Christmas. Casey's "love spell" over me finally broke after I was separated from her for a month. I realized my heart had become neutral when my grandmother asked me if there were any ladies I was interested in and I responded, "You know, there was this one girl I was interested in (Casey), but I don't know if it's going to work out anymore."

> Now ladies, I must chime in here for a moment. I had absolutely no idea Joel was even the least bit interested in me. Throughout the four months of hanging out with him in groups, I continued to guard my heart and thoughts, and simply responded to his pursuit for friendship. Without my knowledge, Joel was trying to determine if a relationship was what he (and God) really wanted. If I had given over my heart, unguarded, it might have been broken if Joel had not chosen to pursue me. But because I guarded my heart, if my friendship with Joel was all the Lord had for us, my heart was completely okay with that.

After Christmas, I flew back to Texas. When I arrived, I started a week-long fast with all the members of the Acquire the Fire ministry team. All the members of the team would meet in the morning to pray together for an hour. On the first day of the fast, in the first time of prayer, I felt the Holy Spirit whisper to me, "I want to speak to you about relationships this week."

I thought it might have just been my mind or emotions playing with me. I prayed even more fervently, "No, God, I'm seeking You this week. All I want is to know You more!" As I continued to pray, surprisingly, I heard the same still whisper again, "I want to speak to you about relationships this week."

I responded, "Okay Lord, if you want to talk to me, I'm ready." Later that week, I recognized a major fear that I had about relationships. Though I was excited to someday find my true love, I had never seen it done successfully before. I had never seen a healthy courtship up close. I was afraid of the unknown. I feared that my relationship would end up like the other toxic relationships I had grown up around. Almost everyone in my family had been married at least two or three times.

As a teen, I had seen examples of relationships that frightened me, even in church. I witnessed some people "fall in love" overnight. One day they were "just friends" and the next they were getting married. I had witnessed some of my Christian friends elope, believing it was a "God-thing," only to divorce a year later.

I needed a different path—a steadier path—than blindly rushing down the road of romance. I wondered how a guy went from hanging out with a girl as a friend in a group to being in a romantic relationship with her. I had never seen this transition done in a healthy way. I needed some sort of rough outline of how to pursue a godly romance, and I needed some simple first steps.

After one of the morning prayer gatherings, I asked Katie Luce, who is like my second mother, if she had some time to stay after and talk for a few minutes. She did, so I asked her what she thought the process looked like for someone going from being a friend in a group to being in a romantic relationship. I knew the emotional power of falling in love with someone could blind even the most clear-minded individual.

Katie said, "The bridge between the two stages is friendship. Before you ever get romantically involved, you have to be best friends first."

It was so obvious and simple. I had never thought of it before, but it made perfect sense. The lights came on. I wasn't sure if I was ready to get romantically involved with anyone, but I knew I could start with being a good friend. And if, in the future, that friendship led us toward romance, I could cross that bridge when it came.

After this conversation, nothing outwardly changed in my and Casey's relationship. We still hung out together in groups, but inside of me, I was growing increasingly interested in getting to know who she was—in a one-on-one setting.

About two weeks later, I was in Houston at a conference where Casey and one of her best friends, Emmie, were working. After one of the sessions, I asked Casey and Emmie out for lunch. Emmie was unavailable, but Casey was.

"Yes," I thought to myself. "Here's my chance." I asked if she would still want to go without Emmie. Casey paused for a moment and then said, "Yes, I would like to."

As I (Casey) mentioned in a previous chapter, I didn't ride in the car alone with guys, so I must admit I was a bit disappointed when Emmie mentioned she could not attend. But when Joel asked if I would still like to join him, it felt as if my heart skipped a beat! A million questions flooded my mind: "Is Joel Johnson really asking me out to lunch? Does this qualify as a date? What about not riding in the car alone with a guy? Would I be breaking my standard?"

Then I thought, "Get a hold of yourself, Casey!" and simply asked the Lord, "God, what should I do?" After I asked, I felt a peaceful, still small voice say, "Yes, you should go." It felt as if I were getting permission from my daddy to go on a date, and boy was I excited! I quickly gathered my things and away we went.

Ron Luce had given me the keys to his silver Infinity G35 and told me I could use it throughout the weekend to get around. I opened up the car door for Casey. She got in, and I shut the door. As I was walking around the car to get in the driver's seat, I whispered under my breath, "Thank you, Papa Luce!"

We took off down the highway. I silently prayed, "Lord help me find the perfect place." We stopped at a quaint, little Chinese restaurant. This was the first time Casey and I had ever hung out alone. I was a little nervous but I was trying my best not to let it show. She looked so beautiful sitting across the table from me. We talked, laughed, and had a great time. I checked my watch and discovered that we had been talking for nearly three hours. When I grabbed the check, Casey asked if she could pay for her meal. I said, "How about I pay for the meal and you can pay for coffee?" She agreed, and I thought to myself, "That was an ingenious move!"

I was also excited about the quaint, little Chinese restaurant Joel discovered. We were the only two in the restaurant at lunch time on a Saturday, which may not say much about the food, but I was sure excited to have a quiet place to talk. We sat at an adorable little table in the back and enjoyed each other's company as the hours passed by. I didn't want Joel to think I expected him to pay for my lunch. After all, this was not an official date, but when he suggested I get the coffee, I must admit that I had never been so excited about buying a "friend" a cup of coffee!

We got back in the G35 and headed off to get some coffee. I pulled into a little diner. They served the worst coffee I had ever tasted, but over that sorry-excuse of a caffeinated beverage, I indulged in the finest conversation I had ever had. Spending time with Casey was so enjoyable!

I looked out the window and noticed it was beginning to get dark. I checked my watch and another three hours had passed! We headed back to the conference.

As I drove home from Houston after the event, I couldn't help but reflect upon the amazing afternoon I had experienced with Casey. We were friends, but we had never connected at such a deep conversational level. I thought, "I'd love to have conversations like that the rest of my life." Talking to her was effortless. It seemed so natural. It seemed we just understood each other.

In the months leading up to this time, we had always hung out in a group setting. I had been impressed with her love for the Lord, self-confidence, wholeness, modesty, strength, love for life, and overflowing joy. I was so happy when I got to enjoy six hours of this, completely uninterrupted!

Like I said, we were friends, but after that day I could see us quickly becoming best friends. We were passionate about so many of the same things: loving God with all our hearts, living life for something greater than ourselves, and passionately pouring our lives into helping the broken and poor. It seemed as if our souls were cut from the same spiritual cloth.

After hours of driving, I finally rolled into bed at 3:00 am. I lay there, staring up at the ceiling, just thinking about the marvelous hours I spent with Casey. And then I had this thought, "Can a guy hang out with a girl for six hours and still just be friends?" I needed to get some counsel. I called Ron the next day.

I drove home from Houston that evening, pondering the amazing afternoon I had with Joel. A million thoughts flooded my mind. I wondered what those six hours meant to him and if he had feelings for me; I certainly knew I had feelings for him. My feet quickly returned to planet earth after the fear set in that he may not like me. I knew that time together equals a relationship and if I continued to spend time with him, my feelings would surely grow.

I felt as if I were at a crossroads. "What if he only likes me as a friend? But what if he likes me more than that?" I knew I could not continue to spend time with him alone without knowing his intentions. At that moment, I surrendered it to the Lord and asked for His direction concerning the relationship. I felt an immediate peace flood my heart as I was reminded that God is my heavenly Daddy and He is looking out for my best interest. At that point, I decided to wait on the Lord for guidance.

I looked to Ron a lot during this time, for several reasons. First, Ron was a friend and mentor. Second, Casey was really close to his family and worked for him, so he knew a lot about her. Third, I had never had a serious "girlfriend" before and was just happy to receive any advice I could get.

When I talked to Ron, I expressed that after spending six hours with Casey I really felt like I needed to communicate to her how I was feeling. I needed to define our relationship and where I hoped it might go. Ron agreed. He talked me through how I planned to communicate my thoughts to her and provided some really great suggestions. (I think I implemented them all.)

I called Casey and asked her if she wanted to go to Barnes & Noble to get some coffee. She asked, "Do you want Emmie to come along as well?"

Thoughts flew through my mind: "Hmm, why did she ask if I wanted Emmie to come? Did she feel differently about our time together than I did? Does she not want to hang out together, just her and me?"

I replied, as cooly as I could, "Well, I don't mind if she comes, but there are a few things I wanted to talk just to you about."

My eyes were shut as I awaited her response. She said, "Okay, great. I just wanted to see." I even detected a little gleeful inflection in her voice as she said it, which I figured was a good sign.

A few hours later, we met at Barnes & Noble.

I was extremely excited and relieved to receive Joel's call that day, but as soon as I hung up the phone, fear gripped my heart again. "What if he does not like me and is going to have a DTR (Define the Relationship) talk with me!

It was a DTR alright; I just didn't anticipate what type! The rest of the day, I was extremely nervous and to be honest a little sick to my stomach at the thought of a humiliating DTR, explaining that he only liked me as a friend.

I got home from work that day and immediately began to get ready. I spent some time with the Lord. I was a nervous wreck and knew I desperately needed His presence to calm my nerves. Then I hopped in my car and headed to Barnes & Noble. Little did I know the conversation I would have with Joel that night would change my life forever.

We walked around the store, talking and looking at different books. We got into the photography section, opened up a book filled with photos of lions and sat on the floor, flipping through the pages. Casey, of course, thought the baby lions were especially precious. I smiled as she talked about their cute furry faces. As I nodded, I remember giving myself a mental pep talk that went something like this, "Alright, Joel, this is the perfect time. You can do this."

As Casey was flipping to the next page, I asked her, "What do you think the progression looks like, going from friends, hanging out in groups, to a more romantic relationship like a courtship? What does the in-between stage look like?"

My heart immediately started racing when Joel said these words. I also felt my face becoming increasingly red. The conversation was definitely different than what I expected, which put a little more hope in my heart. I paused and then said, "Hmm, let me see. It would definitely have to be a relationship centered around God, and you would have to be best friends as well."

I looked into her earnest brown eyes and said, "Well, I would really like to have that kind of a relationship with you." She smiled beautifully and replied, "I would really like to have that kind of a relationship with you, too."

Now, I've never done drugs, but I think I got high right there on the floor of Barnes & Noble. If not, I definitely experienced some sort of significant chemical imbalance! I felt like I was floating! I was a cork bobbing in an ocean of lovely sensations. It was such an emotional surge! Words don't adequately describe how I felt. As Kristen Kappel said, "Love is something you can't describe, like the look of a rose, the smell of the feeling of forever." But whatever it was that I was feeling, all I knew was that I didn't want it to stop.

If Joel was experiencing a "chemical imbalance," he was sure keeping his cool. I, on the other hand, was ecstatic, and I don't think I did as good of a job hiding it. The same thought kept racing through my head, "I am 'friending' JOEL JOHNSON!" I thought at any moment I was going to wake up from a dream!

I shared with Casey what I thought our new season should look like. I suggested that we just continue being really good friends. I said that I'd love to call her three or four times a week and that we'd probably go out to get coffee or something to eat a couple times a week. I also explained that I wanted to keep our physical relationship the same as it had been. We could side-hug, but not for so long that it turned into a "bonafide snuggle." I recommended an approximate three-second limit. I also thought it was good that we not drive alone together after dark.

Now ladies and fellas, I cannot begin to tell you how much Joel's clarification and definition of the relationship meant to me. Oftentimes, girls get lost in a sea of emotions and have no idea what a guy's intentions are for her. When guys do not communicate their intentions clearly, girls are left to guess what the nature of the relationship is, feeling as if the guy likes us when he really might not, and vice versa. It is difficult to find the balance between making yourself available to him, while still guarding your heart.

After my conversation with Joel at Barnes & Noble, there was no confusion in our relationship. I knew Joel's intentions and appreciated the boundaries he gave me. When he called me, came over to my house, or invited me out for coffee, I knew he was genuinely interested in me and was not leading me on. I also appreciated the physical boundaries he set right away. It made me feel valued and respected, but the main reason we chose not to become physical during our friendship stage was to keep our heads clear.

Often, when you become physical with someone, your emotions cloud your judgment and you are no longer able to clearly evaluate that person's character. I thought this was a great plan, and one I felt extremely comfortable with.

I then told Casey, "I don't know if God has anything more for us than this season of becoming better friends. So I think we should enjoy this season that He's given us, but keep our hearts open to God if this season of friendship is all He has for us."

I knew this wasn't the most romantic thing to say, but it was the truth. I had committed to God that I would only move forward as He led me. I had only been given the green light on becoming better friends and I wanted to be transparent with Casey concerning this. I wanted to be very clear so that I wasn't leading her on. She agreed we should just enjoy getting to know each other as friends. I walked Casey to her car and gave her a good night three-second side-hug and said, "I'll call you tomorrow."

Now, I must admit I was a little apprehensive about sharing my heart, emotions, and life with someone who, at this point, only wanted to become better friends with me, but I knew Joel was an incredible guy. Most importantly, he had heard from the Lord, and I appreciated the transparency. I also valued his desire to take things slow, after all this was uncharted territory and both our hearts were at stake.

As I sought the Lord about this new season of my life and my relationship with Joel, I felt the Lord repeat one thing over and over again. "Casey, only allow your heart to go as far as Joel leads. So, if friendship is all he has committed to you, then don't allow your heart to go beyond it."

That's it! That was the key to guarding my heart throughout this relationship. As hard as it was not to allow my mind to wonder what a future would be like with Joel, I instead focused on enjoying Joel's friendship and all that the Lord had in store for us.

Joel and I wanted to take this season of friendship to evaluate if we were right for each other. What I knew of Joel, I liked, but I did not know him well enough to say he was the one for me. Friendship is a perfect time to ask the hard questions of each other and evaluate if that person is your divine match.

Here are some things you should know about each other before moving into a more romantic relationship, like courtship:

- What is your story/testimony?

- What is your family/home life like?

- What are your goals in life?

- What has been your greatest accomplishment thus far?

And so it began, the season we have come to call "Friending." We had a blast! As we talked and got to know more about each other, our friendship flourished. Our conversations grew more and more rich. We hung out in groups and hung out alone together at coffee shops and late night diners.

Casey never pressured me to progress the relationship faster than I felt comfortable. She let me lead. The guidelines we had agreed to, did not make things awkward between us. Surprisingly, they actually made things more fun. Because we had defined the parameters of our relationship, she wasn't frustrated, wondering what my intentions for her were, and I wasn't feeling obligated to move the relationship beyond what I felt God wanted. Our relationship, free to grow within the confines of friendship, flourished. We laughed and enjoyed getting to know each other, no strings attached.

Friendship Is the Foundation

Friendship is the foundation of marriage. It's impossible to have a thriving marriage without it. Building your marriage and life-long romance on anything but friendship is like building your house on the sand. When the storm comes (oh, and they surely will come), your relationship will fall.

Nobody wants to invest years into a marriage that ends in a bitter divorce. Separation or an unhappy marriage is inevitable if a relationship is not based on a foundation of friendship. I'm not saying that you can't develop a friendship after marriage (some people do), but it's much wiser to take some time to see if you can simply be friends before you vow to spend the rest of your lives together as husband and wife.

Some of us have witnessed a relationship that was built on a foundation of friendship. It may have been your parents, grandparents, or maybe an elderly couple in your church. While Joel and I did not grow up with parents who stayed married, we did grow up with grandparents who were madly in love and best friends. I love watching my grandma and grandpa interact over the dinner table. My grandma is the apple of his eye, after all these years. Even as beauty fades, his love for her still remains, because she is his best friend.

There is something to be said about a relationship built on friendship. You see each other through the thick and thin of life, the good times and the bad. You are always there for each other, no matter what storm life may bring. When the beauty fades away, something deeper remains.

Friendship is a matter of the heart. The more you share it with someone else, the closer and more emotionally vulnerable you become. This can bring about an incredible healing in your life, if the other person truly loves you and treats your heart with tender care.

However, if you are vulnerable with a person who does not (or who is not mature enough) to handle your heart appropriately, it can be emotionally and psychologically debilitating. The most risky thing about getting emotionally involved with someone is the nature of feelings that come with it. Of course, the feelings feel really great, but feelings can be very misleading. Somehow our emotions, unfairly influenced by our hormones, make us see only the best in the person we are falling for. Our emotions blind us to their obvious faults and often fill in the unknown about them with rosy optimism.

Often, romantic feelings compel us to give our hearts away prematurely before we even know a person very well. Our emotions can definitely misguide us, which is why we must vigilantly guard our heart. Remember, it *"affects everything you do"* (Proverbs 4:23 NLV). Without serious restoration, a broken heart will affect all your future relationships.

Alfred Lord Tennyson said, "Tis better to have loved and lost than never to have loved at all." Anyone who has ever had to pick up the pieces of their own broken heart after a bitter break-up will tell you that Tennyson was wrong! A broken heart is excruciatingly painful. We must learn to guard our heart and not give it away to just anyone. Regrettably, most people's first stab at love leaves a wound so deep that their heart never fully recovers. As the Sheryl Crow song asserts, "The first cut is the deepest."

My advice is to not let your heart be the laboratory for some rookie's emotional experimentation, because it's likely to go up in flames. There are too many mad scientists running around out there to open up your heart to just anyone. You must guard it!

I'm not saying lock it up and throw away the key. I'm saying that before you share the most tender places of your heart with any potential romantic interest, you must see how he or she treats the less sensitive areas. If this person can't handle them carefully, he or she is definitely not ready to hold the sensitive parts of your heart!

The best arena to find out if a potential life-partner understands how to tenderly care for your heart is in friendship. Ladies, spending time together as friends allows you to see whether your potential "knight in shining armor" is truly a lover and not a fighter, in matters concerning the heart. And fellas, taking the time to be friends will allow you to determine whether your "fox" is truly a kitten and not a cougar in the matters of the heart. (Well, that example may infer more than I intended, but who knows, it may just fit.)

By concentrating on friendship, you'll be able to see how each of you treats the other person's heart and emotions:

- Is what you say kept confidential?

- Does she act one way when you are there, but another way behind your back?

- Does he honor his parents?

- Does she gossip about her friends?

- Does he have a habit of making fun of people?

These are all things you should know before you entrust someone with the deeper portions of your heart, and they are all things you can find out in friendship. Scripture warns us, *"Don't excite love, don't stir it up, until the time is ripe—and you're ready"* (Song of Solomon 8:4).

Being friends with the opposite gender takes some mental and emotional discipline, but it will be worth it for your heart's sake. If a person can be a faithful friend, then they may be able to be a faithful lover. But no one can be a faithful lover without being a faithful friend. In the words of Charles Caleb Colton, "Friendship often ends in love; but love in friendship—never."

Friendship is not only the foundation of marriage, it is also the foundation of romance. Any type of romantic relationship without friendship is shallow. The greatest lovers are the greatest friends. To help solidify this notion, we must turn to some of the most passionate pages in the

Bible: the Song of Solomon. Quite frankly, it says a lot about God that this unbridled book of fiery romance made it into His Holy Scripture.

Though I must admit that every time I read through it I feel a bit voyeuristic, like I've hacked into some couple's private love-blog and am peeping in on their passionate discourse. The lover's exchange is fervent, fanatical, and fiery. Their words are ravishingly raw and risqué. This is some pretty hot and heavy scripture! And it has all the makings of a 21st century romance film. (If Song of Solomon ever made it to the big screen, I could only guess what rating the Motion Picture Association of America would give it—probably not PG.)

It's amazing that God inspired all of this sexually charged poetry and put it into the Bible for us to study. 2 Tim. 3:16 (NLV) says, "*All Scripture is inspired by God and is useful to teach us what is true and to make us realize what is wrong in our lives. It straightens us out and teaches us to do what is right.*" Could God be holding up this couple's unbridled passion as an example of what He desires for every "match made in heaven"? I think so. Why else would He put it in the Bible?

In case you had any doubt before, this book demonstrates that God loves it when a man and a woman are passionately connected—spirit, soul and body in marriage. If God desires us to have what the couple in the Song of Solomon had, then how do we get it? This kind of ardent, authentic love isn't something you see everyday. As La Rochefoucauld lamented, "True love is like ghosts, which everybody talks about and few have seen."

Passionate love and romance can only exist in an atmosphere of friendship. Indeed, friendship is the oxygen of love's flame—without it, fiery passion is extinguished. The couple in the Song of Solomon were not only intimate lovers, but also dearest friends. Expressions of deep friendship entwine throughout their passionate discourse. Just listen to them:

"Oh, my dear friend! You're so beautiful! And your eyes so beautiful— like doves!" (Song of Solomon 1:15)

"A lotus blossoming in a swamp of weeds—that's my dear friend among the girls in the village." (Song of Solomon 2:2)

"Lilacs are exuberantly purple and perfumed, and cherry trees fragrant with blossoms. Oh, get up, dear friend, my fair and beautiful lover—come to me!" (Song of Solomon 2:13)

"You've captured my heart, dear friend. You looked at me, and I fell in love. One look my way and I was hopelessly in love!" (Song of Solomon 4:9)

"How beautiful your love, dear, dear friend—far more pleasing than a fine, rare wine, your fragrance more exotic than select spices." (Song of Solomon 4:10)

"Dear lover and friend, you're a secret garden, a private and pure fountain." (Song of Solomon 4:12)

"I went to my garden, dear friend, best lover! breathed the sweet fragrance. I ate the fruit and honey, I drank the nectar and wine. Celebrate with me, friends! Raise your glasses—'To life! To love!'" (Song of Solomon 5:1)

"I was sound asleep, but in my dreams I was wide awake. Oh, listen! It's the sound of my lover knocking, calling! 'Let me in, dear companion, dearest friend, my dove, consummate lover! I'm soaked with the dampness of the night, drenched with dew, shivering and cold.'" (Song of Solomon 5:2)

"His mouth is sweetness itself; he is altogether lovely. This is my lover, this my friend, O daughters of Jerusalem." (Song of Solomon 5:16 NIV)

"Dear, dear friend and lover, you're as beautiful as Tirzah, city of delights, Lovely as Jerusalem, city of dreams, the ravishing visions of my ecstasy." (Song of Solomon 6:4)

There's no doubt this couple shared one fiery romance, but this romance had a foundation resting on a deep bedrock of friendship. If the Bible is a book of examples of what a supernatural God can do through natural men and women, then the Song of Solomon teaches us that we too can have an amazing God-inspired romance. Undoubtedly, God divinely brought these two lovers together, and He will do the same for you. Romans 2:11 (NLV) says, *"For God does not show favoritism."*

Remember, He is the Divine Matchmaker! He knows your ideal match. God perfectly matched Isaac with Rebekah, and He literally created the perfect match (Eve) for Adam. Song of Solomon exposes God's deep desire for couples to fall authentically and passionately in love.

So how does a man and a woman become (and remain) intimate lovers for life? We call it "friending."

Questions to Ask During Friendship

These are a few questions we received from Ron Luce during our time at the Honor Academy.

1. What is their vision?
2. What are their values?
3. What is important to them?
4. What is their depth with God?
5. Their spiritual strength?
6. How much do they pray?
7. How much do they read their Bible?
8. What significant growth have they experienced over the past year?
9. How are they growing spiritually right now?
10. What challenges are they currently overcoming?
11. What is the biggest or deepest spiritual moment that they have ever had in their life?

    - Was it the moment they got saved or a meeting they went to?

    - What effect has that moment had on their life ever since?
12. Who are their mentors?
13. Who are their favorite authors?

CHAPTER SEVEN

COURTSHIP:

DATING WITH PURPOSE

"Romance is the fuel that keeps love burning hot."
— Rusty Silvey

"Love is when you look into someone's eyes and see their heart."
— Jill Petty

"I had to find you,
Tell you I need you,
Tell you I set you apart."
— Coldplay, "The Scientist"

I had been looking forward to Saturday all week long. I remember it like it was yesterday. Joel had asked me to set that day aside to hang out together. Joel and I had spent the past four months developing an amazing friendship and at the end of those months I could honestly say he had become my best friend. Our hearts had grown more and more fond of each other. It was always a joy to be with him. He not only made me laugh, he also challenged me in my walk with the Lord and my beliefs, and he always had deep questions he would ask to get to know me better.

So, I was definitely looking forward to spending a full Saturday with him. I got up early and began getting ready. Joel arrived at my house early with a basket in his hands. It was delicately draped with a cloth napkin and eggs perfectly placed inside. He prepared breakfast for me at my house as I sat on the counter and enjoyed his company. His scrambled eggs were perfect, accompanied by toast, fresh fruit, and orange juice. I could tell each item was made with care.

After breakfast, Joel whisked me off to Dallas for the day. The two-hour drive seemed only minutes as we laughed and talked the entire way! We pulled up to a beautiful gated area, Joel opened my door and we headed to the entrance of the Dallas Arboretum. As we walked through the entry, I could not believe my eyes. In front of me were the most beautiful gardens I had ever seen. The grass was the brightest shade of green with every type and color of flower you could imagine. The trees were enormous and perfectly groomed with beautiful pathways of stone leading in multiple directions.

We spent hours venturing through all types of gardens and water fountains. We talked for hours about all kinds of things, from our families to our dreams and from our fondest memories of life to our goals. We followed the path around to a beautiful, curious-looking tree in the center of a garden. It had an unbelievably thick branch that jutted, near horizontal, out from its lower trunk. It just so happened to be the perfect height to take a seat and had two drooping bows in it, perfect for sitting on. Joel sat down, and then asked me if I would join him.

We continued to talk, and in the midst of our conversation, Joel asked me what I thought the definition of a courtship was. My heart began to pound a little faster and I could feel the blood rushing directly to my face. The last time Joel asked me a question of this nature, he was expressing his feelings for me. I figured the question would have a good outcome, but could not help but be a little nervous.

After pausing to get my nerves under control, I responded, "It is a relationship with the possibility of marriage." Joel agreed and then said the words I had longed to hear for four months. He said, "I would really like to be in that kind of relationship with you, too."

My heart about leaped out of my chest! Trying not to show my over-enthusiasm, I responded, "I would very much like that." Joel gave me a very warm and affectionate side-hug (this one lasted a bit beyond our 3-second side-hug limitation). We immediately prayed, dedicating our courtship to God, and spent a few moments in awe of our newly entered romance.

We were both starving and Joel suggested we get some lunch. We headed back to his car. I waited as Joel popped the trunk and pulled out a blanket and a wicker picnic basket. He had already prepared lunch, unbeknownst to me. I thought to myself, "Is this guy for real? He is amazing!"

We walked back into the Arboretum and found a perfect place to eat. We sat on a grassy hill overlooking a beautiful lake. It was absolutely beautiful. Joel neatly spread out a blanket over the grass and pulled two speakers out of the basket. He pressed play and Louie Armstrong's *It's a Wonderful World* began to play. He then pulled out two sets of plates, silverware, glasses, and napkins. All the food was neatly prepared and packaged in Tupperware containers. Joel served us and then poured us both some sparkling cider.

After lunch, he gave me a card. I will never forget it. On the cover, in antique coloring, was a coffee cup with a heart in the cappuccino foam. We had enjoyed many cups of coffee together over the course of those four months. Joel had given me many cards throughout those months of our friendship, but this was the first romantic card Joel had ever given me. I opened the card with the utmost care and inside he had written:

Casey,

> You are so special. I cannot tell you how much I enjoy being with you. My life has not been the same since we started hanging out nine months ago—my life is much, much better. You have served me,

encouraged me, and guarded me. You are truly my closest friend. Thank you.

    As we now venture into a new progression of our friendship, I want to say that I am absolutely overjoyed; yet, Casey, I am a bit terrified at the same time. I have never been here before and have never been as vulnerable. So, (deep breath) here is a piece of my heart. Hold it gently, keep it safe and close to yours. If you do, I will give you more.

    Friendship is our foundation—Christ our center—this will never change.

We sat for another hour or so there on the blanket and enjoyed each other's company. We then packed up our picnic and headed back home. Once again, the two-hour drive flew by as we talked over our courtship and what we wanted our relationship to look like.

Joel defined our physical standards and we again reiterated our commitment not to kiss. Joel felt it would be best to put off holding hands until engagement, if the Lord would, ultimately, lead us there. We also felt it would be best not to ride in the car alone together after dark, be at each other's houses past 10 p.m., unless there was a large group of people there.

When we were in public settings, our curfew was midnight. We also felt it best not to be in a house alone together or when people were around to be in a room with the door shut. Some of our friends said our standards were too extreme, but we were committed to not only guard ourselves, but also guard each other's purity and reputation.

Both Joel and I felt that you have one shot at staying pure and we wanted to get it right. We knew that if we got married we could be physical for the rest of our lives. We decided to make these standards to guard each other.

As we pulled into the parking lot of my apartment, Joel mentioned that he had one more surprise for me. He told me to get changed into a dress and he would be back in 45 minutes to pick me up. He then walked me to my front door. I calmly said goodbye and shut the door.

I frantically ran to my room where my roommates were waiting for me. They helped me pick out an outfit and fix my hair and makeup as I told them about my incredible day. Joel was back in what seemed like just minutes and away we went for my next big surprise. After following Joel for approximately 15 minutes (we drove separate cars in accordance with the standards we had just agreed to), we pulled through a black iron gate and up to a beautiful large white two-story home with a wrap-around porch. It was a very well known restaurant in Tyler, Texas called The Mansion on the Hill.

The dinner was wonderful, but I barely ate any of it. I was way too nervous. If Joel was nervous, I couldn't tell because there was nothing left on his plate! A romantic four-course dinner was the perfect ending to what seemed like the perfect day. And that's how Joel led us into our amazing courtship and how the romance of our hearts began.

Leading Up to Courtship

The more I saw Casey's heart during our friending season, the more I was impressed by it. Her wholehearted love for God was arresting. She was way more into Christ than into me. I loved that. Even though she cherished our relationship, she never clung to it (or to me). She seemed entirely satisfied in her romance with God and this passionate love for Jesus translated into a passionate love for life. She oozed cheerfulness; it was infectious.

A permanent smile was plastered on my face whenever she was around. If a "cheerful heart is good medicine," then on several occasions I must have nearly overdosed. I was definitely mesmerized by her physical beauty, but it was her heart that completely captivated me. As Kahlil Gibran noted, "Beauty is not in the face; beauty is a light in the heart." And Casey's heart burned brighter than any other I had ever seen.

After four months of friending, I was more than head-over-heals for Casey. I was falling deeply in love with her. I really wanted to express the romantic feelings I had in my heart toward her and wanted to see if she felt the same way, too. Over the last months, she had held my heart with such tender care that I longed to share more of it with her. She had become my confidant and my closest ally. She was my very best friend and I wanted her to always be in my life.

At this point, I knew we could be friends, but I wasn't sure if we could be lovers of the heart. The only way to find out if we were also romantically compatible was to veer onto a very intimate avenue of friendship—for us to take a stroll down Lover's Lane, but I wouldn't steer our relationship there without hearing from God first.

I headed back out into the field to pray. I asked if God wanted me to enter into a courtship with Casey. I didn't hear anything in response, so I spent some time praising and thanking

God. Then I asked again, "God, do you want me to enter into a courtship?" I still didn't hear a response. I worshiped a little more.

I prayed like this, asking-listening-praising, for about an hour. As the hour passed, I started getting a little more aggressive in my prayers. I passionately asked the Holy Spirit, "What do you want me to do? Should I court her? Lord, you know my will is surrendered to yours." Yet, I received no guidance.

I continued along the same line of questioning for approximately 15 more minutes. "Lord, do you want me to court Casey?" What I heard next totally shocked me.

I heard a quiet, yet direct voice say, "What do you want?" (As in, what do you want to do or what would you like to do?)

I stood there, stunned. It wasn't even remotely close to what I expected to hear. I was expecting a "Yes" or "No," or maybe even a "Hold off for now" or "It's not quite time, my son."

Just month's before, God instructed me to get my will neutral concerning Casey. I fought long and hard to surrender my desire to pursue her and made a pact with God not to make a move without Him ... and now He was asking me what I wanted?!

Why would He ask that after He specifically directed me to surrender? Was He now changing His mind? If I didn't know, at a spiritual gut-level, that God was my heavenly Daddy and that He is always looking to give me the absolute best, then I may have thought God was toying with me. I knew this couldn't be the case. After all the Scripture says:

"Every desirable and beneficial gift comes out of heaven. The gifts are rivers of light cascading down from the Father of Light. There is nothing deceitful in God, nothing two-faced, nothing fickle" (James 1:17).

"No eye has seen, no ear has heard, and no mind has imagined what God has prepared for those who love him" (I Corinthians 2:9 NLV).

Jesus describes the Father as being incredibly generous toward us. He says, *"You parents—if your children ask for a loaf of bread, do you give them a stone instead? Or if they ask for a fish, do you give them a snake? Of course not! If you sinful people know how to give good gifts to your children, how much more will your heavenly Father give good gifts to those who ask him"* (Matthew 7:9).

I was asking for help, and I knew God wouldn't throw a stone or give me a snake instead. (This is why getting to know God and His Word is so critically important in your season of singleness.) God wasn't being cruel or toying with me when He asked me what I wanted.

On the contrary, He was calling me into a great gift that He had divinely set up. "What do you want?" was God's invitation to follow Him into the romance He was orchestrating.

So I asked myself, "Joel, what do you want?" I searched my heart. Was this what I really wanted? With everything in me, I knew it was. I whispered to the Lord, "Yes, I want to court Casey."

I felt a trickle of peace stream through my heart. "Yes, I do want to court her," I said out loud. My heart now welled with joy. Like Abraham's servant, I now knew God—the Divine Matchmaker—was *"working graciously behind the scenes"* to bring Casey and me together. When I said yes to God's question, I was saying yes to enter into the romance He was setting up for me.

That night, I began planning how I would ask Casey if she would like to enter into a courtship.

Courtship Is a Relationship with the Potential of C-C-C-Commitment!

We had not been courting long when Joel flew to New Zealand for three weeks. I knew this would be a trying time for our relationship and I was excited to see if we would weather the storm. We only spoke on the phone twice throughout those weeks, but we exchanged the most precious emails and I can truly say my heart grew fonder of Joel with each email he sent. They say absence makes the heart grow fonder and boy did it!

After Joel returned from New Zealand, he was only home for a day or so and then headed to California for a week. He was scheduled to start school at Pepperdine University in the fall, which left me less than a month with Joel before he moved to California for good.

I did not know how I felt about a long-distance courtship, but I knew Joel was incredible and God was the center of our relationship and

He would guide us through anything. The night before Joel left for California, we met up for coffee. After talking for a bit, he handed me an envelope. I opened it and I noticed a UT Tyler logo at the top left corner. (UT Tyler was only miles from where we both lived.) At the bottom of the paper it said, "Casey, I am reaching for what is important" with an arrow drawn up to the logo. The next page was his fall class schedule at UT Tyler.

I looked at Joel and asked what it meant. He explained that he turned down his near full-ride scholarship to Pepperdine University in Malibu, California. "You are kidding me" I thought to myself. Words could not express the joy that I felt in my heart. I had prepared myself for a long-distance relationship with Joel and the thought of enjoying days with Joel instead of phone calls and emails was almost too much to handle!

I felt as if that was a turning point in our relationship. Beyond all doubt, I knew he was committed to giving our courtship and relationship the best possible chance at success.

Over the next seven months, not only did our friendship flourish, but our romantic feelings for each other did as well. We read through several relationship books and sought out many couples we respected for advice and wisdom, but in the midst of all the recommendations, we wanted to make sure our relationship was our own, not an exact copy of someone else's. We evaluated each opinion and decided what we wanted and what we felt God wanted. We continued to evaluate each other's character throughout our courtship, attempting to always follow the Lord only where He was leading.

WRITE THE VISION

Joel and I are always asked if we broke any of our standards before we got married, and the answer is yes! I will never forget that night: Joel was at my house and we were sitting on the steps leading up to my apartment. It was a well-lit area and my roommates were home. Hours ticked by as we enjoyed each other's company. We were talking and snuggling a bit, too, when we realized the sun was beginning to rise! We had stayed out all night on the front porch!

After Joel left my house, he immediately called Ron, one of our relationship mentors, to explain. I worked as Ron's Administrative Assistant at the time and was nervous all day long, knowing Joel was going to talk to him. After Ron reprimanded both of us, Joel decided it would be a good idea for us to come up with a Courtship Contract, committing to our standards. We presented it to Ron and Katie and asked them for their counsel concerning our standards. The contract read:

> In pursuit of purity, and Christ-likeness, Joel Johnson and Casey Wolston make an open declaration to uphold a principled and disciplined standard of conduct during our courtship. We have prayed, sought council from mentors, received approval from our spiritual covering, and believe the following standards are honorable, wise, and, most importantly, pleasing to our Lord Jesus.
>
> We are, in a disciplined manner, available to lean on each other, put our arms around each other, place our head on each other's shoulder, rest our heads together, and walk arm in arm. We choose not to allow our faces to touch, hold hands, or allow our personal areas to make contact in any way during our courtship. We, as well, will never be alone together in a building, be alone in a vehicle after sundown, be in each other's dwellings after ten p.m. (unless a group or gathering is present), and will never be alone together past midnight.
>
> We not only commit to uphold these written standards during our courtship, but also agree to discontinue any, written or unwritten, activity if we recognize impurity or selfishness arising within.

I printed out three copies of our Courtship Contract and Casey and I signed each copy as a symbol of our commitment to adhere to these standards. Ron and Katie also signed them as a witness of our covenant. Ron and Katie held on to one copy and Casey and I each took one. I had our copies framed so we could hang them up in our rooms. We wanted everyone in each of our houses to know the standards we had committed to. We also knew we needed all the accountability we could get.

Putting our courtship standards into writing was one of the best things we ever did. Having it in black and white helped us map out how we wanted to travel this stretch of our relationship. It cast the vision of what our relationship would look like. As the Lord said to Habakkuk, *"Write the vision. And make it plain on tablets, That he may run who reads it,"* writing our standards gave us a solid vision so we could run this leg of our romantic race in wisdom and purity. As the old saying goes, "If you fail to plan, you plan to fail."

Writing out our physical and emotional standards helped us stay the course even when we were tempted to stray. (We decided to include our courtship standards in hopes that it would serve as a type of rough draft or starting point when it's time to determine your own Courtship Contract.)

THE OTHER SIDE OF SURRENDER

Surrender is not just a commitment not to move without God. It is also a commitment to follow wherever He leads. When it comes to romantic relationships, most people struggle with surrendering their will not to move without God. They get swept up in the flood of feelings, leaving God's council high and dry.

However, surrender is not only refusing to make a move without God, but also following Him wherever He leads. Both are necessary for a divine romance to be successful. God can orchestrate the perfect romance with the perfect person, but if you don't follow God into it, the relationship may just pass you by.

God knows your ideal match. He knows who is best for you, but He will never force you to choose His perfect pick. He let's you choose. If God would never force someone to accept Jesus (even though Jesus is a perfect match for our hearts), then He definitely won't force someone to get married, even if the two people were a perfect match for each other.

God has always respected mankind's decisions, whether good or bad. God didn't stop Adam and Eve's decision to walk away from Him and He won't stop anyone from walking away from a relationship He sets up, no matter how ideal it is. He is more than willing to give guidance, but the final decision is ours to make. He'll lead us to water, but He leaves it up to us to decide if we want to drink.

Abraham and his servant knew that while the Divine Matchmaker would choose a perfect match for Isaac, both Isaac and the undisclosed lady (Rebekah) would have to decide to enter into it. Listen to Abraham and his servant's conversation:

"Abraham spoke to the senior servant in his household, the one in charge of everything he had, 'Put your hand under my thigh and swear by God—God of Heaven, God of Earth-that you will not get a wife for my son from among the young women of the Canaanites here, but will go to the land of my birth and get a wife for my son Isaac.' The servant

136

answered, 'But what if the woman refuses to leave home and come with me? Do I then take your son back to your home country?' Abraham said, 'Oh no. Never. By no means are you to take my son back there. God, the God of Heaven, took me from the home of my father and from the country of my birth and spoke to me in solemn promise, "I'm giving this land to your descendants." This God will send his angel ahead of you to get a wife for my son. And if the woman won't come, you are free from this oath you've sworn to me" (Genesis 24:2-8).

Both the men understood that even though God would guide his servant to Isaac's match-made-in-heaven, no matter how divine the match was, the girl could still decide not to return with the servant to marry Isaac. As we already know, Rebekah chose to enter into what the Divine Matchmaker was coordinating.

"They called Rebekah and asked her, 'Do you want to go with this man?' She said, 'I'm ready to go'" (Genesis 24:58).

Isaac also believed the Divine was at work, after the servant had recounted the miraculous way God had led him to Rebekah. Rebekah freely chose to marry Isaac and Isaac chose to marry Rebekah.

"After the servant told Isaac the whole story of the trip, Isaac took Rebekah into the tent of his mother Sarah. He married Rebekah and she became his wife and he loved her" (Genesis 24:58).

When God asked me, "What do you want?" He wasn't only inviting me into the amazing romance He had planned, He was honoring my freedom to choose. He wasn't going to force anything on me even though it was one of the greatest gifts He had ever prepared for me. He was letting me decide. He was treating me like a friend, like a true son. No, he was treating me like a man.

While I have seen many people rush into a relationship without God's guidance, I have, sadly, witnessed couples be right on the edge of entering into a romance God so carefully crafted for them and one (or both) of them just walk away from it. God won't trespass on your free will. He respects you too much to do that.

If you, like Abraham's servant, are seeking God for guidance concerning a romantic relationship and He clearly gives you some direction, follow Him with a brave heart wherever He leads you. And if the girl is watering your camels, then it might be time to do what Abraham's servant did … give the girl some jewelry!

Questions to Ask During Courtship

These are a few questions we received from Ron Luce during our time at the Honor Academy.

1. Have you seen them upset?
2. What makes them mad?
3. What makes them sad?
4. How do they react under pressure?
5. How proactive are they?
6. Do they really think ahead in their walk with God and plans for their life?
7. What kind of leadership do they take in any given situation?
8. How well thought through are the plans they make?
9. Do you really understand their family situation?
10. What kind of relationship do they have with their father and mother?
11. Did their parents go through a divorce?
12. How close are they to their brothers and sisters?
13. If their parents are still married, are they close to them or do they have a distant relationship?
14. What are the worst hurts from their past? (From who? How did they deal with that in their hearts and how did they deal with that with that person? How did they respond?)
13. What type of personality is the hardest for them to deal with?
14. What annoys them?
15. What are their greatest "life moments"? (How was it pivotal in their life and how did they respond?)
16. What are their greatest successes?
17. What are their greatest failures?
18. Do they have other healthy friendships?
19. Who are their best friends?
20. Are you their only friend?

Personal Questions: It's good to find out a little about their past sexual history. You don't need to know every detail about everything. You don't need to know any names and everything they did, but you need to know their past and their past sexual struggles. Courtship is a relationship with the potential for marriage. Before you ever move forward, you should have at least a general idea. What is shared in this conversaton should be kept absolutely confidential.

CHAPTER EIGHT

THE RULES OF ENGAGEMENT:

SHOW ME THE BLING!

"For a moment like this
Some people search forever …
Oh I can't believe it's happening to me
Some people wait a lifetime for a moment like this."
— Kelly Clarkson, "A Moment Like This"

"Truly loving another means letting go of all expectations. It means full acceptance, even celebration of another's personhood."
— Karen Casey

"Love that is true never grows old."
— Elben Bano

N ow that you've got that bling on your finger, let's get down to a few nuts and bolts. Many couples spend much of their engagement season planning for their wedding and little or no time at all preparing for the rest of their lives together. Then the wedding day comes and goes, the honeymoon ends, and they are wondering what in the world they got themselves into!

The engagement season is not only for planning the wedding, but also for preparing for the rest of your lives together.

You've heard the story of how Joel proposed. Now we want to share some practical advice on how to not only survive your engagement season, but to succeed in the days, months, and years following your wedding. For many, your wedding day will be one of the best days of your life. However, keep in mind that it is only the beginning of your whole lives together.

Your Past Does Not Determine Your Future

As you read in our testimonies, we both came from divorced families, but we made a decision that we would never use the "D" word (divorce) in our home. (You may even want to buy a big dictionary and cut out the "D" word. I know a couple that did that. Divorce is not even in their dictionary, literally!)

In marriage, you will have issues, trials, and problems, but there is no problem or challenge too great for God. He can and will get you through anything. When Joel and I both said "I do" at the altar, we knew we were in it for the long haul. We made a decision that our past did not have to determine our future, and just because we had seen divorce growing up, we no longer had to make that a part of our lives.

No matter what your home life was like growing up, you can establish a different path for yourself. I used to tell myself that I never wanted to have children because I did not want to put them through what I had been through growing up. I was so fearful that I would bring the bad characteristics of my mom and dad into my marriage. After all, if marriage was so good, then why did it not work out for my mom and dad?

It took me many years to realize that this belief was actually a lie. (It was an agreement that I had made with the enemy!) I did not have to have a marriage like my mom and dad's. Instead, I could establish a different path for my future. I knew that with God, *"all things are possible"* (Matthew 19:26 NIV).

Would it take faith and work to live differently? Absolutely, but it is worth it, and it will be worth it for you, too!

While much of your healing from your past must be accomplished during your season of singleness, it is important to renounce and pray over generational curses that might be following you into marriage. You must be aware of potential areas in which the enemy will try to destroy your marriage.

For example, if alcoholism, abuse (verbal or physical), a controlling spirit, infidelity, complacency, or passivity were a part of your home life growing up, it is important to reject those things and make an agreement with God that these will not be a part of your marriage.

Both of our fathers struggled with alcoholism, so we made the decision that we were not even going to allow it into our home. We did not, for one second, want to give the enemy a place to tempt us, so we just decided to not to allow it to be a part of our lives.

I want to encourage you to sit down as a couple and discuss the things from your childhood that you do not want to take into your marriage. Talk about specific areas you struggle with so that you can pray for one another and be aware of how the enemy might be trying to tempt you.

For example, if you grew up with a controlling mom and at times you struggle with control, address the issue, pray, and renounce the spirit of control over your life, then stand together as a couple against the enemy's attack.

You can pray this prayer together:

Heavenly Father, I see and acknowledge the sin and addiction of _____ (your specific area of struggle) that has been on my family. I renounce that sin, addiction, and lie of the enemy over my life. I say that he has no hold over me and that will no longer be a part of my life. I break any and every hold the enemy has over me and say from this day forward it will no longer have a hold on my life, in the name of Jesus. I thank You that I do not have to take the sins of my ancestors into my marriage. The sins of the past are broken in Jesus' name. I pray Your blessings over our future marriage and that our marriage would resemble You and Your church. In Jesus' name, amen

Great Expectations

While I am convinced there is nothing that quite prepares you for merging your life with another person, there are some very practical steps that will provide a smoother transition into matrimony.

For starters, let's talk about the great expectations we carry into marriage! Joel and I learned early on that we must throw our expectations of each other right out the window if we wanted to fully appreciate each other ... and to avoid many fights! When you don't have expectations on each other, everything your spouse does for you is a blessing.

For example, if I don't expect Joel to buy me flowers, take me on a date, or even take out the trash, and he does one or all of these things, I am going to appreciate much more than if I had expected it.

A bit of advice we received from our mentors was to make a list of all the expectations we have for each other, even the basic ones, and then tear it up and throw it away!

For some, you might not even realize the expectations you have on each other. Many of those expectations begin by the way you were raised. Maybe you expect your spouse to take on the roles your mother or father took on when you were growing up.

For example, if your mom cooked, cleaned, and had dinner on the table every night by 5 p.m., you may come into marriage expecting your wife to take on those very roles. Or, if your father worked from 9 to 5, six days a week, while your mom stayed home, you may have those expectations on your husband.

While your parents may have modeled a good example, or even a bad one, it is important to define your parental examples and discuss them with each other.

Here is a little assignment for you that might help eliminate a few fights when it comes to your great expectations.

1. Each of you write down how you see the husband role and the wife role in marriage. For example, what do you think are the wife's responsibilities and what are the husband's responsibilities?

2. Write down the attributes you liked and disliked about your parents' marriage and the particular roles they played in the marriage.

3. How would you like the roles in your marriage to look?

After you write down and define these examples, discuss them with each other.

Define the Roles, But Discard the Expectations

While it is important to define the roles you will play in marriage, it is important to discard those expectations. For example, the house is my responsibility (to cook, clean, organize, do the laundry, and go grocery shopping), but if Joel comes home and the house in not clean, he does not get upset or angry with me. When he comes home and the house is clean, dinner is cooked, and the house is in order, he is thankful because it was a blessing to him and not an expectation on me.

When Joel and I were engaged, we discussed all the responsibilities of marriage and decided our roles. We decided that Joel would be the provider of our family and that I would continue being a full-time student. Joel has always been a great provider, but if times got hard, I was more than willing to take on a full or part-time job. While that is the role Joel fills, I always try to show my appreciation for his provision and never expect it of him.

When your roles are defined, but the expectations of each other are discarded, you will enjoy marriage and each other all the more.

Show Me the Money!

The number one reason for divorce is money! Many couples assume their money problems will just disappear after marriage, but sadly, many discover a pile of debt that appears soon after the wedding bells ring.

It is important to get on the same financial page before you say "I do." While I am not a financial expert, and recommend you read books specifically on finances, I want to share a few basic things to get you started.

#1 Set up a budget

There are plenty of helpful tools out there to guide you, but it is important to get on the same page when it comes to where your money goes. Joel and I made the decision that I would be a full-time student while he worked, so we set our budget on what we could afford based on his income. Joel would be the primary breadwinner of our family, and if I chose to work, my income would go straight to savings.

We made this decision so that if we were ever in a difficult position, we would A) have money in savings and B) I could pull up some of the slack during a difficult time.

The largest piece of advice I could give you while setting a budget is to live within your means. We live in a society that is defined and categorized by material things, but for the sake of your marriage, do not buy into that lie. Instead, make the decision and commitment to always live within your means. If you do this, you will save yourself much heartache in the future.

Here are a few categories to consider while setting up your budget:

1. Tithe (10% of your income) This must come first before anything else.
2. Rent (What is an affordable monthly payment?)
3. Food
4. Utilities
5. Car Payments (Are you paying cash or getting a loan?)
6. Insurance
7. Miscellaneous
8. Personal Money

#2 Merge your bank accounts

A piece of advice we received during our engagement season that we found to be helpful was to merge our bank accounts. After setting our budget, we began using the same account to get us used to what it was going to be like after marriage.

There are so many transitions you face after marriage, making the big merge ahead of time can help things after you say "I do." You are able to work out any glitches and you are able to adjust to your budget that you set.

#3 Discuss your financial baggage

It is also important to discuss any debt or loans that you have prior to entering into marriage, such as credit cards or school loans. It is unfair to withhold that information until after you say "I do." The amount of debt you have can be a heavy weight on your marriage and you need to go into it with eyes wide open.

You should also discuss your credit scores with each other. Once again, this is something that not only can affect your marriage for years, but it also says a lot about how you handle your money. If you or your spouse have a poor credit score, you may be unable to obtain a loan for a car, house, or possibly even a school loan.

Also, if there is a lack of discipline when it comes to the way you spend your money, these issues need to be addressed now, because they will lead to larger problems in the future.

HANDLING THE IN-LAWS

When you marry your special someone, you are not only marrying them, but (in some ways) their family as well! For some, this is a blessing, and for others, it is a curse. Interacting with your in-laws can be like walking a tightrope, but hopefully we can offer a few tips that will help you navigate this sometimes rocky terrain.

First things first: we must leave our mother and father and unite with our spouse (Matthew 19:5). For some of you, leaving your parents and uniting with your mate is a simple concept, no problems there! You were itching to get out of the house the day you turned 18! But for others, especially us ladies, it is often easier said than done.

When you are married, your parents are no longer your covering. For a man, you are now under God's covering and for a woman you are now under the covering of your husband, financially, spiritually, and emotionally. What this means is that you are now to unite, bond, merge, blend, and come together. The emotional needs your mother or father once met are now available for your husband or wife to meet.

Now, I am not saying that you cut off your relationship with your parents. Rather, I am saying that your relationship with them will change after marriage.

Let me give you a few examples of how you will leave your parents and unite with your spouse. For starters, when there is a conflict between the two of you, never go to your parents to resolve it (unless you are in a dangerous situation, such as physical abuse, etc.). While you may forgive him in an hour or so, it will more than likely take your parents much, much longer.

I don't know about you, but my mom always has my back and it would probably take years for her to forget about a disagreement I had with Joel if I had discussed it with her. Every time she saw Joel she would be thinking, "How dare you hurt my daughter!"

Now, I am not saying that you just keep your disagreements between the two of you because it is important to find a mentor or accountability partner you can confide in and help you through certain things, but this is information that should not be shared with your parents.

I understand this can be challenging. If you are like me, you tell your mom everything, but your marriage is simply off limits. If you share the conflict going on in your marriage with your mom or dad, your most certainly put your relationship with your spouse in jeopardy. There are a select few parents who will remain objective, but they are few and far between. Most will develop an opinion about your husband and immediately take offense at his actions. The same applies to you husbands!

In our time traveling the country together, Joel and I met a sweet couple whose marriage was in complete shambles. Let's call them Bob and Sally. They are a great, bad example:

> Bob is extremely close to his mom and confides in her about everything. His mom is his biggest cheerleader, greatest supporter, and no matter what he does wrong, she is always there to encourage him.
>
> When Bob was 10 years old, this was a wonderful thing, but now that he is 40 and married with children, it has created a few problems. His wife, at times, is not as enthusiastic about his major mistakes, which drives him to go to him mom instead of his wife.
>
> Bob is struggling with leaving his mother and uniting emotionally to his wife. And while Sally feels left out and isolated from the relationship, Bob's mom is growing increasingly angry toward Sally. Bob can do no wrong in her eyes, and Sally is to blame for every fight, disagreement, and trial that comes their way.

Now, this is not only unfair to Sally, but Bob is selling their marriage short. Instead of going to his wife to solve their problems, he is getting his emotional needs met by his mother. Until Bob learns to face his challenges with his wife and leave his mother out of it, he will continue to fight about the same problems and miss out on the wonderful emotional connection he could have with Sally.

There will be times in every family, no matter how great your parents are, when conflicts emerge. Joel and I have a rule that we each deal with our own parents. If there is a conflict with my mother, I am the one who handles it, and vice versa.

For example, if Joel or I have done something to upset my mother, I am the one who speaks with her and handles the misunderstanding. This can be extremely difficult to do, especially if my mom has done something to hurt Joel. But, for the sake of a future relationship, it is important to address issues as they come up, and it is best to deal with your own parents when it comes to conflict.

LET'S TALK ABOUT SEX

I cannot end this chapter without addressing an issue that will be a very big part of your marriage ... sex! However, for the sake of those who are nowhere near ready to address this issue, I will remain vague, only addressing the most important matters, and encourage those of you who are engaged to get further counsel from your mentors and premarital counselor on this topic.

In addition, I recommend that you discuss the issues I am about to address approximately one month before your wedding day. You don't want to awaken love before you say, "I do," and believe me, you will need every ounce of strength to stay pure during this season.

Joel and I chose to discuss these issues a few weeks before our actual wedding day to make sure we remained pure and did not awaken anything by discussing the topic of sex. So, let's dive right in.

For starters, it is good to get on the same page when it comes to sex. For example, talk about what you are comfortable with, without being graphic or inappropriate. It is important to respect and honor one another in this area, so if you're soon-to-be spouse is uncomfortable with something, it is important to discuss this ahead of time and honor that request.

Also, talk about your fears regarding sex. Both Joel and I were virgins and I felt much better after talking to Joel about some of the fears I had concerning having sex for the first time. The most helpful advice I can give you is to meet with a married couple (separately, of course) who you feel comfortable with and who are honorable, respectful to each other, and Christians, and discuss this topic with them.

Even if you have had sex in the past, it is important to get a godly, pure perspective from a married couple. I personally met with my mentor whom I greatly respected and trusted. She answered all my questions, calmed my fears, and gave me some very practical advice for my honeymoon!

Last, but certainly not least, you must address your physical standards during your engagement season. Joel and I both found that the engagement season was the most difficult season to remain pure. Your engagement season is like being married without the benefits of living and sleeping together. You are madly in love while deciding on a place to live, talking about things that you may have never talked about, and making plans to spend the rest of your lives together! Naturally, your physical body wants to follow your heart.

If there is ever a time to beef up those physical standards it would be now. After all, you are almost there! What a shame it would be to make it through your entire dating season, remaining pure, and then mess up during your engagement. I remember a friend of mine tell me that they literally had to sit on opposite sides of the couch just to remain pure!

Joel and I decided to keep the same physical standards as our courtship season, however, we allowed ourselves to hold hands during this time, which I very much enjoyed! If you notice yourself slipping or being tempted more than usual, raise your standards for a time and make sure you have as much accountability as possible. You are on the downhill stretch and you are almost there. No matter how difficult it may be, you can do it!

While you are always growing and looking for ways to improve your marriage, my prayer is that this chapter will help you start off running at full speed. If you implement the advice given in this chapter, you will indeed thrive. And remember to have fun with the assignments in this chapter and your engagement season!

CHAPTER NINE

THE DIVINE MATCHMAKER:

GOD IS ENGAGED

"I'll be a personal guide to them, directing them through unknown country. I'll be right there to show them what roads to take, make sure they don't fall into the ditch."   — Isaiah 42:16

"He spoke to me in the voice so sweet
I thought, I heard the shuffle of the angel's feet
He called my name and my heart stood still
When He said, 'John, go do my will.'"
          — Johnny Cash, "God's Gonna Cut you Down"

"They know exactly what to do and when to do it. Their God is their teacher."   — Isaiah 28:26

Whether we know it or not, God is engaged. He is actively involved in our world and intimately involved in our lives. Jesus said,"*The man who enters by the gate is the shepherd of his sheep. The watchman opens the gate for him, and the sheep listen to his voice. He calls his own sheep by name and leads them out. When he has brought out all his own, he goes on ahead of them, and his sheep follow him because they know his voice*" (John 10:2-4 NIV).

What stands out to me in this passage is that the Shepherd (Jesus) "*goes on ahead of them.*" What a reassuring thought! Jesus actually goes ahead to guide us through life. (He intimately knows each one of us and He calls us "*by name.*") I don't know about you, but for most of my life I felt like I was on my own. I believed the Shepherd wanted the best for me, but it was up to me to make it all happen. "You must happen to life or life will happen to you," was the internal mantra, playing over and over in my mind like a song stuck on repeat. I viewed life like a big, ever-accelerating steamroller, and if I didn't want to become road-kill, I had to keep moving … make it happen, blaze my own trail, and become a self-made man! I was a sheep without a shepherd and I was exhausted.

For those of us who have lived this way, it's a result of seeing God not as the close friend He is but as someone who is distant and far away. It's that orphaned spirit I described earlier. It's a lonely and exhausting way to live. The transition to a better life starts when we believe God is actively and intimately involved in our lives on a daily basis. That He's engaged!

If we choose to follow the Shepherd, He promises to lead us to "*real and eternal life, more and better life than they ever dreamed of*" (John 10:10). Knowing that God is intimately engaged in our lives and that He goes before us to lead us into a life beyond our dreams can provide particular reassurance, especially when it comes to our love life.

Let's face it, trying to find true love can be a precarious endeavor. If you're single, you live in dangerous dating country. Often hiding behind a stallion, stud, or fox exterior is a cougar, wolf, or man-eater. (Watch out, they'll chew you up!) These predators are poised to pounce on any unsuspecting prey. They lick their chops just thinking about sinking their teeth into another muttony heart. They fancy to feast on a particular species known as "sheeple" (part sheep, part people).

Sheeple suffer from shortsightedness, lack of foresight, and gullible disposition, which makes them easy prey. In addition, sheeple walk alone where the wild things are; there, predatory wolves gleefully wait to gobble down these sheeple like ten-year-old boys tearing into a bag of mini-marsh-mallows.

If you're single, you know it's a jungle out there. When your heart is at stake, you can't afford to try and find love all by yourself. We truly need the Divine Matchmaker to shepherd us through the current romantic terrain.

Jesus warned, *"Let me set this before you as plainly as I can. If a person climbs over or through the fence of a sheep pen instead of going through the gate, you know he's up to no good—a sheep rustler! The shepherd walks right up to the gate. The gatekeeper opens the gate to him and the sheep recognize his voice. He calls his own sheep by name and leads them out. When he gets them all out, he leads them and they follow because they are familiar with his voice … I am the Gate. Anyone who goes through me will be cared for—will freely go in and out, and find pasture. A thief is only there to steal and kill and destroy. I came so they can have real and eternal life, more and better life than they ever dreamed of"* (John 10:1-4, 9-10).

Much like the current dating scene, the environment these sheep lived in was perilous. It was filled with predators, phony shepherds, and thieving sheep-nappers. The only way for the sheep to stay safe was to stay close to their true shepherd. The sheep *"recognize his voice"* and *"he leads them and they follow because they are familiar with his voice."* If they followed the shepherd, they would find life and pasture, but if they wandered off on their own, they exposed themselves to many perils.

Now, believing that the Shepherd can lead you into a life beyond your wildest dreams is a start, but believing this alone will not keep you safe from the lions, tigers, and bears! These beasts are constantly on the prowl *"looking for some [stray] victim to devour"* (I Peter 5:8 NLV). Nor will it protect you from the thief who seeks to *"steal and kill and destroy."* In order for you to remain alive in the dangerous land in which you live, you must know the Shepherd's voice and follow His lead.

If you hadn't noticed, Jesus compares us to the nearsighted, unin-telligent livestock—sheeple! This is not a messianic slight on the human race, but rather, it's a sober caution. Warning us that we live in enemy-occupied territory, and compared to the strength and intelligence of our enemies, we are—without the Shepherd—as vulnerable as Mary's little lambs.

We were never made to live life on our own. We were created to live in a loving conversational intimacy with God. One of the biggest decisions you'll make is the person you are going to marry. God wants to shepherd you through the process of finding that person.

If you want help from God, the Divine Matchmaker, then learning to recognize His voice and follow Him wherever He leads is essential. If you believe God goes before you, leading you into a life beyond your dreams, that is good, but holding this belief does not insure your safety from the prowling predators who seek to do you harm. To be safe, you have to stick close to the Shepherd. Without the Shepherd, your heart is as good as lamb chops.

So, if you don't want any ol' heartbreaker, dream-maker, or love-taker to mess around with your heart, it is imperative that you learn to hear the Divine Matchmaker's voice and follow His lead.

Hearing God's Voice: Know He's Speaking

Hearing God's voice is something we learn. It's like everything else in life we really enjoy doing, it takes time and practice to get good at it. Think about snowboarding, playing guitar, basketball, singing, chess, football, dancing, gymnastics, and even video games. It takes time and effort to get proficient at any one of them, but once you get the hang of it, it's a blast!

It's the same process with learning to hear God's voice. Hearing from and talking with God is one of the most enjoyable things we will ever do in life, but it takes time and practice. Here are a few of the fundamentals.

God loves to talk

The first thing you must know is that God loves to talk and that He can't get enough of talking to human beings. He speaks to people all throughout the Bible. God spoke to Adam *"in the cool of the day"* (Genesis 3:8 NIV). He spoke to Moses *"as a man speaks to his friend"* (Exodus 33:11 NIV). He spoke to Abraham, Sarah, and even to Sarah's banished maid, Hagar (Genesis 18:13-15, 16:13). He told Peter what to eat, He talked to

Paul about repentance, and He commanded fearful Ananias to pray for the newly repented Paul (Acts 10:13-15, 9:4, 10-15). The Lord spoke to Samuel, Noah, Gideon, Elijah, Elisha, and the list goes on!

He even advised David in the smaller details of life, like moving. *"After all this, David prayed. He asked God, 'Shall I move to one of the cities of Judah?' God said, 'Yes, move.' 'And to which city?' 'To Hebron'"* (II Samuel 2:1). If God spoke to David even about the smaller matters, like where he should relocate, then you should be encouraged that He'll speak to you about one of most important decisions of your life: who you should marry!

Scripture leaves little room for us to doubt that our Father in heaven loves to talk to His kids on earth.

The Father

When our first child, Lincoln, was born, I would talk to him all the time. I would say all sorts of things that dads say, like, "How you doing Little Buddy? Lincoln, you're such a good boy! Daddy loves you!" I couldn't help but vocally express to him how much he meant to me. I knew he didn't understand a single word I was saying, but I really didn't care. I just loved to communicate my heart with him, even though our communication was mostly me talking to him and him smiling or cooing back at me.

I knew that when Lincoln got older we could have a conversation where he understood what I was saying and could tell me what was on his mind. But even though he couldn't do this as a baby, I couldn't help but continuously shower him with loving words. I was obsessed with talking to him!

Now, if I am totally preoccupied with communicating with my child, imagine how much more our heavenly Father is preoccupied with talking to us? As Jesus said, *"If you sinful people know how to give good gifts to your children, how much more will your heavenly Father ..."* (Matthew 7:9). If I, being a sinful person, love talking to Lincoln, how much more does our perfect Father love talking with us?

John 1:12 says, *"Yet all who receive him, to those who believe in his name, he gave the right to become children of God"* (John 1:12). If you are His child, you had better believe He's speaking to you, whether you can understand His words yet or not, He's hopelessly showering you with loving expressions. In other words, He is a father and He is totally obsessed with talking to you!

Psalm 139:17-18 says, *"How precious are your thoughts about me, O God! They are innumerable! I can't even count them; they outnumber the grains of sand!"* Mathematicians at the University of Hawaii estimated that there are seven quintillion five quadrillion (7,500,000,000,000,000,000) grains of sand on the world's beaches. That is a lot of thoughts, especially considering that if people live to be 80 years old, they only live for approximately two billion, five hundred and twenty-four million, six hundred and eight thousand (2,524,608,000) seconds.

Here's the breakdown:

80 years = 29,220 days (not including leap years)
29,220 days = 701,280 hours
701,280 hours = 42,076,800 minutes
42,076,800 minutes = 2,524,608,000 seconds

Now, that might not seem very exciting, but consider that if all of God's thoughts toward you occurred during your entire lifetime, He would have approximately:

93,750,000,000,000,000 thoughts about you every **year**
256,673,511,293,630 thoughts about you every **day**
10,694,729,637,235 thoughts about you every **hour**
178,245,493,954 thoughts about you every **minute**
2,970,756,233 thought about you every **second**.

That's almost 3 billion precious thoughts about you every second! And what really blows my mind is that Psalm 139:17-18 (NLT) says His thoughts for us actually *"outnumber the [7,500,000,000,000,000,000] grains of sand!"* His thoughts for us are *"innumerable"* (Psalm 139:17 NLT).

The Son

I think it's safe to say that God thinks a lot about each one of us. How could our heavenly Dad not want to express some of the quintillions of thoughts He has about us directly to us? Isn't that the reason the Father sent His only Son, to communicate His love? (John 3:16). Colossians1:15 tells us *"We look at this Son and see the God who cannot be seen. We look at this Son and see God's original purpose in everything created."*

Jesus came to echo just how much our heavenly Daddy loves us. Jesus said, *"I've let you in on everything I've heard from the Father"* (John 15:15). All the hours Jesus spent teaching and healing on earth were to communicate to us just how much our Father loves us and wants to fully heal us from our brokenness.

Jesus spoke and people's hearts and bodies were restored. Peter described Jesus as the One who had *"the words of real life, eternal life"* (John 6:68). The book of John calls Jesus the Word: *"So the Word became human and lived here on earth among us."*

God loves speaking to us so much that He actually came in human form, through Jesus Christ. Truly, God is obsessed with talking with His kids. Jesus lived and died to communicate just that.

The Holy Ghost

God's ability to communicate with us—intimately and personally—only increased when Jesus left the planet. Shortly before Jesus ascended into Heaven, He said, *"It is actually best for you that I go away, because if I don't, the Counselor won't come. If I do go away, he will come because I will send him to you"* (John 16:7 NLT).

If Jesus was God's Word in the flesh and His disciples could clearly hear Him speak, then we can at least expect that His Spirit will speak to us as clearly as Christ did. Jesus said that when the Spirit came it would be to our *"advantage"* (John 16:7 NKJ).

Jesus said that the Spirit's words would be so unmistakable that His followers shouldn't even prepare a defense when they were persecuted. He said, *"Just say what God tells you to. Then it is not you who will be speaking, but the Holy Spirit"* (Mark 13:11 NLV). He promised His followers that they would be able to hear the Spirit speak clearly, so clearly that they could then repeat the words He gave them. He assured His disciples that *"The right words will be there. The Holy Spirit will give you the right words when the time comes"* (Luke 12:12).

Jesus also said that His Spirit would counsel us. He said, *"And I will ask the Father, and he will give you another Counselor, who will never leave you"* (John 14:16 NLV). This perfect Counselor would help navigate us through life. Jesus articulated that *"when the Friend comes, the Spirit of the Truth, he will take you by the hand and guide you into all the truth there is. He won't draw attention to himself, but will make sense out of what is about to happen and, indeed, out of all that I have done and said"* (John 16:13).

Jesus promised that the Spirit would lead us intimately, hand-in-hand, into all that is true. This Counselor is *"the Spirit of Him who raised Jesus from the dead [who] dwells in us"* (Romans 8:11 NKJ).

Our heavenly Father speaks His thoughts to His children, intimately and instantly, through the Holy Spirit who lives in us. *"For who among men knows the thoughts of a man except the man's spirit within him? In the same way no one knows the thoughts of God except the Spirit of God"* (I Corinthians 2:11 NIV). The Spirit knows God's thoughts and lives within us and we can be sure that He is lovingly speaking those thoughts to us.

The Spirit also prays for us, listens to us, and shares the Father's good thoughts with us (Romans 8). What else would you expect from a perfect Counselor?

Know that God wants to talk with you. Intimate communication is at the heart of a personal relationship with God. Isn't that what humanity lost in the garden? A close intimate friendship, walking and talking with God?

I know this may be difficult for many of us who grew up going to Sunday school to believe, but the reason Christ came to earth was not to die on a cross for our sins. The reason He came was to restore humanity's broken relationship with God. Christ dying on the cross was part of the costly price God paid in order to restore that relationship.

The Good News isn't that we can now go to church, read our Bibles, and pray. (The Pharisees had this routine down better than most of us ever will.) The Good News is that we can have a personal relationship with God, and that means intimate communication with the Divine. If we desire, we can know God's thoughts through His Spirit, and that's especially good news because *"No eye has seen, no ear has heard, no mind has conceived what God has prepared for those who love him—but God has revealed it to us by his Spirit"* (I Corinthians 2:9-10 NIV). God wants to communicate with you, and I know He has some really good things to share.

Hearing God's Voice: Talk to Him, Listen to Him

To hear God's voice better, we must internally slow down, quiet ourselves, and patiently pursue the Lord in prayer. That means we talk to Him and then listen to Him.

I Kings 19:11-12 says, *"'Go out and stand before me on the mountain,' the LORD told him. And as Elijah stood there, the LORD passed by, and a mighty windstorm hit the mountain. It was such a terrible blast that the rocks were torn loose, but the LORD was not in the wind. After the wind there was an earthquake, but the LORD was not in the earthquake. And after the earthquake there was a fire, but the LORD was not in the fire. And after the fire there was the sound of a gentle whisper"* (NLV).

Though the Lord speaks to people in various ways, like Elijah in this passage, I find that He most often speaks to me in a quiet tone. His words always bring peace and life. Even when His words are corrective or convicting, they are never condemning. *"Therefore, there is now no condemnation for those who are in Christ Jesus,"* says Romans 8:1 (NIV).

It's in the quiet steady place of my soul that I usually hear Him speak. It's this place that I must connect with. The place where my heart is calm, open, and at rest. As God recommended, *"Be still, and know that I am God"* (Psalm 46:10 NIV). It always takes me slowing down and getting quiet to connect with Him there.

How I get to that "still" place is always a little different for me. Sometimes I lock myself in my office and pray in silence, sometimes I get up early have some coffee and read the Word, or I go to Starbucks and pop in my headphones and listen to worship music as I journal. The goal is to open up my heart to Him. I ask Him a question (or write the question, if I'm journaling) and then pause to listen for that still small voice to speak. I usually repeat the question if I don't hear anything in my heart. I'll tell the Lord how great He is and quote scriptures that reinforce that He speaks, loves, and is faithful to respond to His children. I also often repeat the question as I wait for a reply.

I know God hears me the first time I pray, but I do this mostly to help me concentrate. (My mind wonders quite easily when I pray, so repeating the question helps me focus.) If I have condemning, negative, lustful, wacked-out, or ungodly thoughts, I cast them down in Jesus' name and usually quote a few scriptures that rebut the lying thought with the truth (II Corinthians 10:5).

Let me give you an example. If I'm praying and I have a thought that comes into my mind that says, "I'm on my own. It's up to me to figure out how to make life work."

As soon as I recognize the thought, I say, "I don't believe that lie. I make no agreement with it. I cast that thought down and choose to make an agreement with what God's Word says! He says that He *'never leaves me nor forsakes me'* (Hebrews 13:5) and *'Every good gift and every perfect gift is from above, and comes down from the Father of lights, with whom there is no variation or shadow of turning'* (James 1:17 NKJ). That means that my heavenly Dad never leaves me and that there is no dark side to my Dad. He is always good and gives me perfect gifts! I am not on my own. I have been adopted and His Spirit lives in me (Ephesians 1:5, Galatians 4:5, Romans 8:15). I am blessed with every spiritual blessing in the heavenly realms because I belong to Christ! (Ephesians 1:13)."

I will pray any other scriptures that come to mind, or if I need to see what the Bible says about something in particular, I'll run a word search for some scriptures on www.crosswalk.com or www.biblegateway.com.

When I am asking God for direction or requesting something from Him, I try not to stress out if I am not hearing anything. If I feel God is bringing up another issue beside the one I am asking about, I go down that road. The Father knows our need even before we ask Him (Matthew 6:8). I try to keep the attitude Jesus described we should have when we ask the Father for something:

> *"What I'm trying to do here is to get you to relax, to not be so preoccupied with getting, so you can respond to God's giving. People who don't know God and the way he works fuss over these things, but you know both God and how he works. Steep your life in God—reality, God-initiative, God-provisions. Don't worry about missing out. You'll find all your everyday human concerns will be met. Give your entire attention to what God is doing right now, and don't get worked up about what may or may not happen tomorrow. God will help you deal with whatever hard things come up when the time comes"* (Matthew 6:31-34).

I attempt to stay in this attitude, knowing that *"everyone who asks receives; he who seeks finds; and to him who knocks, the door will be opened"* (Matthew 7:8 NIV). Being expectant and persistent that God will answer our prayers, yet being patient as we ask, seek, and knock, is the balance of heart I try to have when I approach God with a request.

The book of James also describes this type of expectant, enduring and patient type of prayer:

> *"The earnest prayer of a righteous person has great power and wonderful results. Elijah was as human as we are, and yet when he prayed earnestly that no rain would fall, none fell for the next three and a half years! Then he prayed for rain, and down it poured. The grass*

turned green, and the crops began to grow again" (James 5:16-18 NLV).

What first strikes me about this scripture is that James is trying to drive home the point that God doesn't just answer super-spiritual people's prayers. He will answer the prayer of anyone who is in right standing with Him (of course, praying in accord with His will). He emphasizes this by saying the Prophet Elijah *"was as human as we are."*

The second thing that pops out at me is that He uses the story of Elijah praying for rain. Elijah was expectant that God would respond to His prayer, yet prayed with persistence until He did:

> *"Elijah climbed to the top of Carmel, bowed deeply in prayer, his face between his knees. Then he said to his young servant, 'On your feet now! Look toward the sea.' He went, looked, and reported back, 'I don't see a thing.' 'Keep looking,' said Elijah, 'seven times if necessary.' And sure enough, the seventh time he said, 'Oh yes, a cloud! But very small, no bigger than someone's hand, rising out of the sea....' Things happened fast. The sky grew black with wind-driven clouds, and then a huge cloudburst of rain..."* (I Kings 18:42-45).

Even the great prophet, Elijah, had to pray with patient persistence to receive an answer to prayer. He sent his servant back seven times before he saw anything that even resembled a rain cloud. Likewise, we shouldn't get discouraged if God doesn't respond instantly to our prayers. Pray with patient persistence like Elijah did, even if it takes seven times!

We need to practice slowing down, quieting ourselves, and then patiently pursuing the Lord in prayer. Talk to Him and then take the time to listen.

Hearing God's Voice: Know His Word

Another part of hearing God better is to read, memorize, and meditate on scriptures. The Bible is a written record of God's interaction with mankind. In it we see God's thoughts, desires, ideas, emotions, and the back-and-forth communication He had with different people over the centuries. I find this fascinating because in many ways the Bible is much like a blog or social networking site.

When we open the Bible, we have the opportunity to see God's postings and get to read other people's comments and replies. As you explore His profile, you quickly see that God's friends list is immense! He has friends from all social classes and demographics and time periods. Through the Bible, we can view God's chats with leaders of ancient super-powers, teenagers, ultimate fighters, prophets, priests, and slaves. Through the thousands of posts and comments throughout history, we begin to know God better.

We see what He likes and dislikes, what makes Him glad, sad, or angry. We discover what He says, how He says it, and to whom he says it. For example, when God encounters a hypocritical religious leader, you may see a response like, *"Snakes! Sons of vipers! How will you escape the judgment of hell?"* (Matthew 23:33 NLT). If you're weary, worn-down, or disillusioned, you'll read a reply that looks something like this. *"Are you tired? Worn out? Burned out on religion? Come to me. Get away with me and you'll recover your life. I'll show you how to take a real rest"* (Matthew 11:28).

Through the Bible, we find out a lot about the Divine and how He communicates through His countless posts, replies, and comments. The more familiar we are with His profile, the more likely we will be able to recognize His voice when He speaks directly to us. Discerning God's voice is the very skill that we'll need if we're going to successfully follow the Divine Matchmaker to our true love.

Let me illustrate the point:

Imagine if a friend from school introduces you to a really good friend of his via facebook, my space, xanga, or one of the other various social networking sites. Even though the guy didn't post a picture of himself (which I personally find irritating), you still send a "friend request" anyway and he accepts.

Once you've gained access to his page, the first thing you notice is that his friends list is the largest one that you've ever seen. Then you start reading through some of his older posts and discover this guy is a pretty fascinating individual. He's been all over the world and knows all sorts of people—celebrities, heads of state, social workers, television evangelists, movie stars, politicians, philosophers, physicists, and, interestingly, he even hangs out with some boy-band members.

The more you read through his different conversations, message threads, and comments, the more you like him. You begin to feel like you actually know him and wished you really did know him better. You start visiting his page almost every day because he always has something entertaining, intriguing, or really interesting to read. You can tell he's intelligent, bright, talented, and wealthy, but you really enjoy how down-to-earth he is. Every time you visit his profile, you feel like you discover something totally revolutionary about him or about life in general.

Then one day as you were exploring his page, you happen to discover that he's a world-renowned matchmaker. He's done it for years and has the highest match success rate on the planet. You also discover that he is willing to help anyone of his online friends for free!

You can't believe what a coincidence this is because you've found yourself wondering how and if you would meet that special someone. You've never thought of using a matchmaker before and at first you're a little uneasy with the thought. But then you think, "This guy knows a lot of great people, so maybe he could introduce me to at least one or two potentials."

So you search his photo albums and discover he has matched millions of people together. As you peruse page after page of the glowing, embracing couples he has matched, you can't help but think that you would like to be posted in one of those photos some day. You begin to believe that if this guy could help all these people find their match, that maybe he could help you find yours, too.

You seriously consider contacting him. You check his profile information and discover that he's listed his phone number (something I don't recommend). At first you think, "Oh, I won't call him. I'll just send him a message or an email." But unable to resist the temptation of getting the matchmaking process started immediately, you grab your cell phone, dial his number, and press send.

It rings four times and, regrettably, goes to voice mail. You leave a very excited message, inquiring about the use of his services and then end the call. You write a post on your wall: "Can't believe I just called a matchmaker today! Left him a voicemail. I hope he calls back. I promise I'm not desperate, just really, really interested!"

Later that evening you get a phone call from a guy who says he's the matchmaker. You pour out your heart to him, describing intimate details about yourself and what you are looking for in a spouse.

At the end of the phone call you discover that it wasn't the matchmaker, but rather your coworker, Eddie, who has recorded your conversation and is now threatening to post it online if you don't take a few of his late-night work shifts. He said he read your post and just couldn't pass the opportunity up.

You receive several other bogus "matchmaker" phone calls like Eddy's throughout the rest of the night. You begin to wonder how you'll ever know if it's the true matchmaker calling you back.

The following afternoon, you receive a call from an unlisted number—the person on the other end says he is the matchmaker. At first, you are quite skeptical, wondering if it's really him speaking to you or if it's just another imposter. But as you listen to him, you recognize that everything he says lines up consistently with what you've read on his site. He sometimes even quotes himself word-for-word and responds very much like his online replies, conversations, comments, and message threads. You're familiar with what he's written and it clues you in that it's really him, the true matchmaker!

You recognize the Divine Matchmaker's voice in much the same way. When you're familiar with God's writing, it also clues you in that it's really God speaking to you. The more you read and memorize God's Word, the more it helps you recognize and distinguish His voice from all the other competing voices and thoughts vying for your attention.

The Bible is a written record of God's interaction with mankind. In it we see God's thoughts, desires, ideas, and emotions, not to mention the dialogue He had with His different friends over thousands of years. Through the Bible we find out a lot about the Divine and how He communicates. It's our primary resource in learning to identify and distinguish His voice from our enemy's (the imposter's voice) and our own thoughts.

The more familiar you are with God's writing, the more it will clue you in that it's really Him, the Divine Matchmaker, speaking to you!

You must remember that hearing God's voice is something you learn. It takes time and practice to get good at it. Also, always remember that God loves to talk to you!

Spending time in persistent prayer and reading the Word are some of the fundamentals we must put into practice in order to grow in our ability to hear God better. We desperately need God's guidance to and through the process of finding true love. Practicing these fundamentals will help us "sheeple" hear and follow our Shepherd much better.

If you are new to hearing God, may I suggest that you start by asking Him to speak to you about something less life-altering than your future mate. Start by asking God about the day-to-day stuff and keep a record of what you hear and what happens. Record what the fruit or results of your actions are. Jesus recommends that we judge things according to its fruit (Matthew 7:18).

Also, if the written Word says it plainly (i.e. *"Do not lie."* (Leviticus 19:11 NIV), then you don't have to ask. You already know what His will is.

I would also recommend that you read *Walking with God*, by John Eldredge. It's been a valuable resource to Casey and me in learning to hear God better and discover just how actively and intimately God is engaged in all our lives.

Lastly, I recommend that you pray this prayer (or something close to it) regularly:

Father, I want to hear You better. I confess that I can't make it through life without Your guidance. I turn from trying to make it on my own. I know that You want to intimately guide me through life. Wherever You guide me, I want to follow. Thank You for calling me by name. Help me to hear. I am listening. Holy Spirit, perfect Counselor, teach me to hear better. I want to follow You into the life and the love life You have prepared for me. Your will be done, in the name of Jesus, amen.

CHAPTER TEN

THE DIVINE MATCHMAKER:

WISDOM AND REVELATION

"After he called them by name, he set them on a solid basis with himself. And then, after getting them established, he stayed with them to the end, gloriously completing what he had begun."
— Romans 8:30

"Ya know He's doin' it?
Yo, who's doin' it?
God is doin' a new thang!"
— (Old School) DC Talk, "New Thang"

"No one who trusts God like this — heart and soul — will ever regret it."
— Romans 10:11

P aul prayed, "*I keep asking that the God of our Lord Jesus Christ, the glorious Father, may give you the Spirit of wisdom and revelation, so that you may know him better*" (Ephesians 1:17 NIV). We need both God's written wisdom and conversational revelation to follow the Shepherd into the life that He promised was beyond our dreams.

Whether this is your first trip down the road of romance or you've made prior attempts, it's time to let the Divine Matchmaker get involved. He's the expert on love—the original Love Guru.

Involving wise principles in your romance is good, but involving God's principles along with the Wisest Person Ever in your romance is much, much better. There's no doubt, if we are going to follow the Divine Matchmaker, we must yield to His written wisdom and guiding revelation.

WISDOM

"*If you become wise, you will be the one to benefit. If you scorn wisdom, you will be the one to suffer*" (Proverbs 9:12).

God's wisdom and timeless principles are necessary to successfully travel down the road of romance. Wisdom guides us down the right route of relationships, it guards our hearts and bodies, and it serves as a gauge to help us evaluate where we are and how we are doing.

Learning wisdom concerning romantic relationships is incredibly beneficial because it not only keeps us safe before we get married, it also guides us safely throughout our entire lives. Wisdom is our guide, guard, and gauge, keeping us safe for a lifetime as we travel the road of romance. However, if you scorn wisdom, you will suffer.

Think about King David. From his youth, he was a champion for God. As a teen, he had faith to slay giants. He had open conversations with the Lord like this one: "*It was reported to David that the Philistines were raiding Keilah and looting the grain. David went in prayer to God: 'Should I go after these Philistines and teach them a lesson?' God said, 'Go. Attack the Philistines and save Keilah'*" (I Samuel 1:1-2).

Besides being a warrior, David was also a musician and songwriter. He wrote many of the beloved psalms in the Bible. David, ultimately, united the 12 tribes of Israel and ruled as their king. God loved and adored David, so much so that He called David *"a man after his own heart"* (I Samuel 13:14 NIV).

But after decades of faithfully walking with God, David chose to ignore the Lord's principles and guidelines concerning romantic relationships. Although the Lord loved and favored David, that did not make David immune to the consequences of disdaining wisdom. What David thought would be a romantic stroll down Lover's Lane turned into a four-lane, 400-car pileup! The repercussions of his romantic wreck troubled David for the rest of his life.

King David was having an ongoing sexual affair with Bathsheba. When Bathsheba became pregnant, he wanted to marry her, but there was one major obstacle hindering this ... Bathsheba was already married. Her husband, Uriah, was a faithful husband and a devoted soldier in David's army.

At first, David tried to cover up his affair by bringing Uriah home from the battlefield, but Uriah, ever the faithful soldier, wouldn't sleep with his wife. He said, *"The ark and Israel and Judah are staying in tents, and my master Joab and my lord's men are camped in the open fields. How could I go to my house to eat and drink and lie with my wife? As surely as you live, I will not do such a thing!"* (2 Samuel 11:11 NIV). Even after David pushed to get him drunk, Uriah still wouldn't sleep with his beautiful bride, Bathsheba.

Unsuccessful in his attempt to cover up his affair, David sent Uriah back to the battlefield with a plan to eliminate him. David commanded his generals to *"put Uriah in the front lines where the fighting is the fiercest. Then pull back and leave him exposed so that he's sure to be killed"* (II Samuel 11:15). Everything went as David planned—Uriah died and David married Bathsheba. It looked like they were going to live happily ever after.

But scripture says, *"God was not at all pleased with what David had done"* (II Samuel 11:21). God sent the prophet Nathan to tell David what the result of breaking God's wise guidelines for romantic relationships would be. Nathan said, *"'And now, because you treated God with such contempt and took Uriah the Hittite's wife as your wife, killing and murder will continually plague your family. This is God speaking, remember! I'll make trouble for you out of your own family ... You did your deed in secret; I'm doing mine with the whole country watching!' Then David confessed to Nathan, 'I've sinned against God.' But because of your blasphemous behavior, the son born to you will die"* (II Samuel 12:10-14).

David spent weeks repenting, fasting, and praying, but it did not change the outcome of what David's decisions set in motion. He had blatantly scorned wisdom and was reaping its vicious results. The newborn died and David was publicly embarrassed. His selfish actions wounded the rest of his family as well.

Later on, we see that many of David's kids were angry, insecure, vain, and had little respect for him. Incest, rape, murder, and treason all plagued David's home, just as the prophet Nathan had predicted!

Clearly, God's wisdom, principles, and relational guidelines give us clearly-defined rules to protect us from the potential relational wrecks that can happen over a lifetime.

David's son, Solomon, witnessed the countless troubles his father faced in the aftermath of his affair with Bathsheba (Solomon's own mom). Solomon didn't hold back on warning his people against sexual immorality. In Proverbs 5:1-14, Solomon warned the young men in his kingdom: *"Dear friend, pay close attention to this, my wisdom; listen very closely to the way I see it. Then you'll acquire a taste for good sense; what I tell you will keep you out of trouble. The lips of a seductive woman are oh so sweet; her soft words are oh so smooth. But it won't be long before she's gravel in your mouth, a pain in your gut, a wound in your heart. She's dancing down the primrose path to Death; she's headed straight for Hell and taking you with her. She hasn't a clue about Real Life, about who she is or where she's going. So, my friend, listen closely; don't treat my words casually. Keep your distance from such a woman; absolutely stay out of her neighborhood. You don't want to squander your wonderful life, to waste your precious life among the hardhearted. Why should you allow strangers to take advantage of you? Why be exploited by those who care nothing for you? You don't want to end your life full of regrets, nothing but sin and bones, Saying, "Oh, why didn't I do what they told me? Why did I reject a disciplined life? Why didn't I listen to my mentors, or take my teachers seriously? My life is ruined! I haven't one blessed thing to show for my life!" Never Take Love for Granted."*

Solomon knew that if his father—a man after God's own heart—could disregard God's ground rules for relationships, he knew that anyone could. It dearly cost his father, his family, and the kingdom. Solomon warned that the short-term pleasure sexual immorality may bring is not worth squandering your whole life for. He knew that if his father, the king and a man of God, could not escape the consequences of ignoring wisdom, then no one could. He had seen the devastating impact it had on his dad and warned the people of his kingdom not to follow the same route.

Solomon concluded his admonition in Proverbs 3 by declaring: *"Why would you trade enduring intimacies for cheap thrills with a whore? for dalliance with a promiscuous stranger? Mark well that God doesn't miss a move you make; he's aware of every step you take. The shadow of your sin will overtake you; you'll find yourself stumbling all over yourself in the dark. Death is the reward of an undisciplined life; your foolish decisions trap you in a dead end"* (Proverbs 3:20-23).

God wants us to choose wisdom in our relationships in order to keep us from romantic wrecks and a dead-end life. There is nothing that will get you there faster than sexual immorality. I Corinthians 6:18 says it plainly: *"There is a sense in which sexual sins are different from all others. In sexual sin we violate the sacredness of our own bodies, these bodies that were made for God-given and God-modeled love...."* The NLT version says that *"sexual immorality is a sin against your own body"* (I Corinthians 6:18).

One of the reasons the Bible gives us so many guidelines concerning romance (and why Casey and I set such high standards) is that romance can be so emotionally intoxicating. These feelings can definitely turn you around and make driving the wrong way feel like it's right. As *Dead or Alive* noted, romantic feelings have a way of spinning you "right 'round like a record, baby, right 'round, 'round, 'round."

Emotions can make you morally dizzy, a state you don't want to be in while driving down the road of romance. Sexual immorality is more life threatening than driving on a four-lane freeway in the wrong direction. Why? Because it has the potential to not only kill your body, but also your soul and spirit! The Bible warns, *"There's a way of life that looks harmless enough; look again—it leads straight to hell"* (Proverbs 14:12). The road of sexual immorality always leads to death—the ultimate dead end.

Just like a driver's safety manual outlines the rules of the road to keep everyone safe, so God's Word outlines the rules of the road for romance to keep you safe as well. If you travel by road (like most of us do), you're glad that people generally stop at red lights, adhere to the speed limit, and don't drive while drunk. Following these guidelines gets people where they want to go, safely and successfully.

God's relationship guidelines do the exact same thing for our heart, spirit, and body. So, if God's guidelines for the romantic road tell you when to stop, how fast you should go, and prohibits driving while emotionally intoxicated, you should be glad. The guidelines are the method to get you where you want to go, safely and successfully. If you ignore them, like David and Bathsheba did, a major collision is inevitable.

Remember, Proverbs warns that *"If you scorn wisdom, you will be the one to suffer,"* but if you follow God's relationship guidelines and *"become wise, you will be the one to benefit"* (Proverbs 9:12 NLT). If you choose to follow God's wisdom, principles, and rules of romance, you're on your way to a safe, sane, and successful journey down the road of romance.

SOME WARNINGS ABOUT WISDOM

Now, I'd like to give a quick warning about wisdom. While God's Word compels us to pursue wisdom, it also warns us not to lean on it apart from the Lord. Proverbs 3:5-6 says, *"Trust in the Lord with all your heart, And lean not on your own understanding. In all your ways acknowledge Him, And He shall direct your paths"* (NKJ). I like how The Message version says it: *"Trust God from the bottom of your heart; don't try to figure out everything on your own. Listen for God's voice in everything you do, everywhere you go; he's the one who will keep you on track."*

The wise rules and principles He has given us in the Bible are a great gift to us. They give us the framework in which God acts. He will never act contrary or ask us to do something contrary to what's written in His Word. This is incredibly helpful, especially if you're trying to hear God's voice in the midst of a flood of romantic feelings.

But thank God He has gone way beyond just handing us a list of rules and principles and hoping we'll be strong enough to follow them! God really wants us to lean on Him as He personally guides us through the process. He designed us that way. Remember, He is the vine and we are the branches, apart from Him we can do nothing (John 15:5).

God said that when we wholeheartedly trust and lean on Him that He would actually *"direct"* us, that if we listened to His voice, He would *"keep [us] on track!"* Isn't this what we really need? Not just a record of rules, but also a friend who will help us stay the course each step of the way?

Paul prayed, *"I keep asking that the God of our Lord Jesus Christ, the glorious Father, may give you the Spirit of wisdom and revelation, so that you may know him better"* (Ephesians 1:17 NIV). The Spirit that helps us know God better does so through wisdom and revelation. We need them both to hear and follow our Shepherd wherever He leads.

Like I said before, whether this is your first trip down the road of romance or you've made prior attempts, it's time to let the Divine Matchmaker get personally involved. If you do make this decision, you must remember that while God is a person of principle, He himself is not one. God is a person, not a principle. God is not a formula and there aren't any precise formulas for those who follow Him. We were never made to lean on our *"own understanding"* apart from God. John Eldredge said, "God is a person, not a doctrine. He operates not like a system—not even a theological system—but with all the originality of a truly free and alive person."

Principles are a tutor that educate us about God and His ways (which are indispensable), but it is far better to have His friendship than principles alone. Jesus said, *"I'm no longer calling you servants because servants don't understand what their master is thinking and planning. No, I've named you friends because I've let you in on everything I've heard from the Father"* (John 15:15).

When it comes to God and your love life, it's best to exchange stale formulas for an informal friendship. Expect God to act with all the originality of a truly free and alive person, because He is.

Let God Do a New Thing

"This isn't a variation on the same old thing. This is new, brand-new, something you'd never guess or dream up. When you hear this you won't be able to say, 'I knew that all along'" (Isaiah 48:7).

The miraculous way that God brought Isaac and Rebecca together shows us that God is infinitely interested in your love life and desires to supernaturally connect you with the true love of your life.

While this is undeniably true, Isaac and Rebecca's love story (or anyone else's for that matter) is unique. You cannot make a principle out the details of someone else's love story. The secret is to remain open to letting God coordinate your love story in a brand new way. God is alive, creative, and totally original! He is always devising new ways to do things.

Have you ever noticed how He never arranges a major event in the Bible exactly the same way twice? Think about the walls falling at Jericho, Gideon defeating the Midianites, David killing Goliath, manna falling from heaven, or the virgin birth, God never orchestrates events like these the exact same way twice! (Jesus was much the same way. He was always coming up with an original way to heal blind people.)

God is totally original, and you must be open to let Him be completely original in orchestrating the details of your love story.

Boaz and Ruth let God do an original thing in their romance. Boaz was a distant descendant of Isaac and Rebekah. Undoubtedly, he was quite familiar with the details of how God divinely matched Isaac with Rebekah, but Boaz was open to letting God make his love story a complete original.

One night, as Boaz was sleeping out in the fields near his freshly harvested wheat, he suddenly awoke to find a woman resting at his feet. The woman had done this *"to signal her availability for marriage"* (Ruth 3:7). He asked, *"And who are you?"* (Ruth 3:9) The woman replied, *"I am Ruth, your maiden; take me under your protecting wing. You're my close relative, you know, in the circle of covenant redeemers—you do have the right to marry me"* (Ruth 3:9).

Now, if Boaz had turned the details of his ancestor's experience into a principle, he may have thought that Ruth should have never pursued him in this manner. (After all, Rebekah did not pursue Isaac this way.) Instead, Boaz said, *"God bless you, my dear daughter! What a splendid expression of love! And when you could have had your pick of any of the young men around. And now, my dear daughter, don't you worry about a thing; I'll do all you could want or ask. Everybody in town knows what a courageous woman you are—a real prize!"* (Ruth 3:10-11).

If Boaz, a direct descendant of Isaac and Rebekah, was willing to let God write his love story in an original way, then so should we!

God's hand can be seen in bringing both Isaac and Rebekah together and Boaz and Ruth together, but the way He orchestrated the details of each was quite different. God never arranges a major event in the exact same way, and your love story is one of those major events! It's a huge deal! And you can expect the Divine Matchmaker to orchestrate it in a totally original way! As Oswald Chambers said, "Never make a principle out of your experience; let God be as original with other people as he is with you." There's no doubt that God divinely coordinates marriages, but how He goes about doing that will always be entirely unique.

Yes, we must travel the road of romance adhering to God's wise principles. This keeps our hearts, bodies, and spirits safe as we journey, but in order to follow the Divine Matchmaker into the unique romance He is orchestrating for you, you must trust the Lord to direct you and not make principles out of what others have experienced. As Proverbs 3:5-6 says, *"Trust in the Lord with all your heart, and lean not on your own understanding. In all your ways acknowledge Him, and He shall direct your paths"* (NKJ).

Another ancestor of Isaac and Rebekah's was Joseph, Mary's husband. What if he had tried to make a principle out of what God had done for his ancestors? What if he had followed God's wise principles (leaning on his own understanding) and not trusted in the Lord with all his heart? He would have missed out on the unique love story the Divine Matchmaker was orchestrating for him and Mary. (He would have also missed out on an amazing opportunity to raise the Savior of the World!)

When Joseph appears in scripture, He was already engaged to Mary. Things seemed to be running smoothly as the couple neared the big wedding day until Joseph discovered that Mary was pregnant. He knew he hadn't done anything that would qualify him as her "baby's daddy," so he planned to do what most guys would do if they were in his position: dump her.

Matthew 1:18-24 explains: *"Before they came to the marriage bed, Joseph discovered she was pregnant. (It was by the Holy Spirit, but he didn't know that.) Joseph, chagrined but noble, determined to take care of things quietly so Mary would not be disgraced. While he was trying to figure a way out, he had a dream. God's angel spoke in the dream: 'Joseph, son of David, don't hesitate to get married. Mary's pregnancy is Spirit-conceived. God's Holy Spirit has made her pregnant. She will bring a son to birth, and when she does, you, Joseph, will name him Jesus—"God saves"—because he will save his people from their sins.' This would bring the prophet's embryonic sermon to full term: Watch for this— a virgin will get pregnant and bear a son; They will name him Emmanuel (Hebrew for 'God is with us'). Then Joseph woke up. He did exactly what God's angel commanded in the dream: He married Mary."*

Joseph knew God's relational guidelines and he had every scriptural right to abandon the relationship, but Joseph refused to lean on principle apart from God. He was open to follow wherever God would lead, and when Joseph received some divine guidance telling him that Mary was in fact his intended match, he married her. Joseph was unwilling to make a principle out of anyone's past experience. Literally, God had never done this before. The Immaculate Conception (virgin birth) was something totally new!

(Now guys, remember, God doesn't usually do the same thing twice, so if your fiancé tells you she somehow immaculately conceived and there's no way you could be responsible, I would suggest getting some DNA testing done to verify her story.)

The birth of Christ was a major event and the Divine Matchmaker was outdoing Himself to make it wholly original. Joseph could have followed every scriptural principle and guideline perfectly, but if he didn't also heed the counsel of the Divine Matchmaker, he would have missed out on his match-made-in-heaven. (He probably would have also gone down in history as the guy who dumped the Savior of the World's mother, a label no man would want to bear. Listening to God definitely paid off for him!)

Like Joseph, you must be open to how God wants to craft your relationship. Listening to and following God's counsel is a necessary part of discovering your match-made-in-heaven. God sincerely wants to guide you with as much clarity as He gave Joseph, both to and through the process of finding your divine match!

JACK AND JILL

Not long ago, an old friend came over to our house. (We'll call her Jill.) It was great to see her as it had been years since we had all connected. Jill, in her early 30s, was still single. During her 20s, she had two or three serious relationships that all ended just short of matrimony.

Over a cup of hot tea, Casey and I asked how she was doing and were curious if anything was going on in her love life. She said that she was really interested in a guy she had been friends with for years, but he wasn't making any moves to pursue her. She explained that they got along great and had a blast together, but she couldn't figure out why he wasn't pursuing her on a more romantic level. "I don't know what to do," she confessed. "Should I wait for him, or move on?"

She was trying to listen to God's voice, but she wasn't hearing anything concerning what direction she should take. She was willing to wait like Rebekah (have God supernaturally bring a man from a distant land to offer his hand in marriage) or go the way of Ruth (telling him of her "availability for marriage"). She was willing to do whatever the Lord desired. She was asking and asking, but wasn't hearing Jack.

I really felt for her. Most of us have been in the exact same position at one time or another—asking God for divine direction and not hearing a thing or not knowing what you heard was God's voice or your own thoughts. It's a very unpleasant place to be.

As she was talking, I felt like God wanted to speak to her about it. I asked her if Casey and I could pray with her and see if God would speak to one or all of us about it. As the three of us prayed, I felt like God was saying that He didn't want her to go the way of Ruth. In fact, I had a very strong impression that she should not approach the gentleman she was interested in about entering into a romantic relationship.

I expressed what I heard in my heart to her and Casey and tears began to run down Jill's face. She said that she really felt the Lord was speaking the same thing to her. Casey agreed with Jill, saying she also had the same impression. All three of us felt like the Lord was guiding her not to communicate her romantic interest until this guy first pursued her.

Jill was determined to trust God in this, and she left our house that night with a deep sense of peace and joy. She trusted that if the Lord wasn't requesting her involvement that He was more than capable of planning her love story on His own.

Not long after, Casey and I received an e-mail from Jill. It said:

"I also wanted to let you know that totally out of the blue (the guy I was telling you about) ended up coming down and going to a concert with me, staying at my mentor's house and we had a great time. He wants to see where "this" can go. I've been coming down from the high of it all and really pressing into the Lord for His voice, direction, etc. I am hopeful, but no matter what happens, I feel like this is the biggest test of my life regarding guarding my heart, stewarding my emotions, holding and waiting, trusting God, and NO MATTER what happens, I want to pass this test and never go around and around this mountain again."

Listening for God's voice requires you to go beyond embracing His principles and all the way into embracing God as a Person. Hearing God's voice necessitates that you seek out a personal relationship with Him. God has given you His wise principles to guide you, guard your heart and body, and help you gauge how you are doing. But God wants more. He wants relationship. He wants to personally guide you into a life better than you could have dreamed (John 10:10).

Your Match Made in Heaven

God is the ultimate matchmaker. He knows everything about you, and everything about everyone, and even knows your perfect match. He's truly working behind the scenes to match you up with the right person. It's only logical that you ask Him for help uncovering who that person is? It worked out well for Isaac and Rebekah, Ruth and Boaz, Mary and Joseph,

Adam and Eve, the lovers in Song of Solomon, and countless other couples throughout time.

And undoubtedly, it will work out well for you, too.

As you know, Casey and I followed God's matchmaking advice and it worked out wonderfully for us. He brought us together and we can never adequately express our gratitude to Him for this.

We hope that the Divine Matchmaker's time-tested tips, secrets, and wisdom that we've shared will help you as God guides you down the road of romance. We really hope you'll choose to give the Divine Matchmaker a call. There's no one who's been at it longer or Who is better at it than He. However, if you do choose to let Him orchestrate your love story, remember, that though His principles on love are timeless, He never brings two hearts together the same way twice.

Just as it became clear that Rebekah was Isaac's divine match when she attended to the servant's thirsty camels, we pray that your divine match becomes clearer as you attend to the guidance in the Scripture and these chapters.

Sometimes it takes a lot of time and energy to make sure that God is *"working graciously behind the scenes,"* but as Rebekah learned, those camels she repeatedly tended to were *"loaded with gifts from [the] master"* (Genesis 24:10).

Here's to your match made in heaven!

To order other Divine Matchmaker resources or to contact Joel and Casey, please visit:

www.thedivinematchmaker.com

Scriptures to Put to Memory

Psalm 139:14 "Oh Yes, you shaped me first inside, then out; you formed me in my mother's womb. I thank you, High God- you're breathtaking! Body and soul, I am marvelously made! I worship in adoration- what a creation! You know me inside and out, you know every bone in my body; you know exactly how I was made, bit by bit, how I was sculpted from nothing into something. Like an open book, you watched me grow from conception to birth; all the stages of my life were spread out before you, the days of my life all prepared before I'd even lived one day."

Psalm 119:73 (Amplified) "Your hands have made me, cunningly fashioned and established me; give me understanding, that I may learn Your commands."

1 Samuel 16:7 "But God told Samuel, "Looks aren't everything. Don't be impressed with his looks and stature. I've already eliminated him. God judges persons differently than humans do. Men and women look at the face, God looks into the heart."

1 Peter 3:3-4 (NLV) "Don't be concerned about the outward beauty of fancy hair styles, expensive jewelry, or beautiful clothes. You should clothe yourselves instead with the beauty that comes from within, the unfading beauty of a gentle and quiet spirit, which is so precious to God."

Proverbs 31:30 (NLT) "Charm is deceptive, and beauty does not last; but a woman who fears the Lord will be greatly praised."

Psalm 17:8 (NIV) "Keep me as the apple of your eye; hide me in the shadow of your wings."

Purity Commitment Form

     I (write your name) _____ commit to emotional, physical, and sexual purity from this day forward (write today's date) _____. I choose to save my heart and body for the person God has for me until marriage.

     I have forgiven myself for any past mistakes that I have made and realize God has also forgiven me. I receive the Lord's forgiveness and from this day forward, I commit to purity. I will save myself for marriage.

_____

(Your signature)

_____

(Your accountability partner's signature)

Questions During Friendship

These are a list of questions we received from Ron Luce during our time at the Honor Academy.

1. What is their vision?
2. What are their values?
3. What is important to them?
4. What is their depth with God?
5. Their spiritual strength?
6. How much do they pray?
7. How much do they read their Bible?
8. What significant growth have they experienced over the past year?
9. How are they growing spiritually right now?
10. What challenges are they currently overcoming?
11. What is the biggest or deepest spiritual moment that they have ever had in their life?

   - Was it the moment they got saved or a meeting they went to?

   - What effect has that moment had on their life ever since?
12. Who are their mentors?
13. Who are their favorite authors?

Questions During Courtship

These are a list of questions we received from Ron Luce during our time at the Honor Academy.

1. Have you seen them upset?
2. What makes them mad?
3. What makes them sad?
4. How do they react under pressure?
5. How proactive are they?
6. Do they really think ahead in their walk with God and plans for their life?
7. What kind of leadership do they take in any given situation?
8. How well thought through are the plans they make?
9. Do you really understand their family situation?
10. What kind of relationship do they have with their father and mother?
11. Did their parents go through a divorce?
12. How close are they to their brothers and sisters?
13. If their parents are still married, are they close to them or do they have a distant relationship?
14. What are the worst hurts from their past? (From who? How did they deal with that in their hearts and how did they deal with that with that person? How did they respond? What did they say?)
13. What type of personality is the hardest for them to deal with?
14. What annoys them?
15. What are their greatest "life moments"? (How was it pivotal in their life and how did they respond?)
16. What are their greatest successes?
17. What are their greatest failures?
18. Do they have other healthy friendships?
19. Who are their best friends?
20. Are you their only friend?

Personal Questions: You need to find out about their past sexual involvement. You don't need to know every detail about everything. You don't need to know any names and everything they did, but you need to know their past and their past sexual struggles.

Notes to Self

Notes to Self

Notes to Self

Notes to Self

Notes to Self

Notes to Self

Notes to Self

NOTES TO SELF